Celestial Navigation by H.O. 249

Celestial Navigation by H.O. 249

by

JOHN E. MILLIGAN

Cornell Maritime Press

Centreville   Maryland

Library of Congress Cataloging-in-Publication Data

Milligan, John, 1913-
  Celestial navigation by H.O. 249

  1. Nautical astronomy.   2. Navigation.   I. Title
VK555.M57   623.89   74-1464
ISBN 0-87033-191-4

Manufactured in the United States of America
First edition, 1974; eighth printing, 1994

CONTENTS

INTRODUCTORY NOTE

In the summer of 1971 there were two boat arrivals on the east coast of the Island of Oahu that puzzled me. The first was a sailboat from California in the 35-40-foot range that was home-built and crewed by a half dozen or so young people of college age. When interviewed by a local reporter and asked how they had found their way, the skipper answered that they had used a ten-dollar transistor radio with some directional qualities, and had started west by a little south sailing until they picked up Honolulu radio stations, and then homed in on them. They had had no other navigational equipment except a compass.

A few months later a sort of home-built motor sailer arrived at the same coast from Oregon. This boat did not have even a transistor radio. Stereo equipment was aboard but it had used up all their power on the way down. In answer to the same question put to them by a reporter, they answered that they had followed the direction indicated by the contrails of high flying aircraft headed this way.

This made me wonder how many missing youths from the mainland have tried and failed to make it here.

I began thinking of the need for a manual on navigation which was simple enough for the novice to grasp and complete enough for him to find his way if he had collected what he needed before he started. This book is a result of that concern. If it will save but one, it will have been worth the effort.

The Author

CELESTIAL NAVIGATION FOR THE BEGINNER

A rogue comber, more rambunctious than the regular ranks marching steadily down from the north, smacked into the hull not four inches from my face as I slept in the quarter berth. The half inch of fiberglass between me and the sea reverberated with the blow, and I heard cries of anguish from the cockpit as the crew on watch was baptized in the brine. I squirmed from the berth, rubbed the sleep from my eyes and peered out the hatch. The motion of the boat had already let me know, as I awakened, that the sea was still up. It had been so since the start of the race some three days before. The winds had been reported at 35 knots, and as we had been through it, I was not about to argue with the reports. What I was really interested in, however, was not the sea, but the sky. We had been boiling along recording over eight knots on a close reach since the evening of the first day. Problems with steering had required the use of two helmsmen on the wheel for most of the time. A bad leak through the rudder post had drowned out our engine, and as a result we would probably be without electric power soon. This would mean no lights, and no log to record the miles run. I had not seen the sky since the start and wanted a fix badly; not a heroin fix—a celestial fix.

My spirits rose as I studied the heavens astern through the main hatch. The solid gray overcast that had prevailed all the way from the coast was deteriorating. A crosshatch of irregular lines, lighter than the dull gray, gave proof that the sun was really up there somewhere and promised a break soon. No longer sleepy, I grabbed my sextant from its box and hurried on deck. As I watched, the sky thinned further, and a sharp round ball of light soon appeared behind the remaining screen of cover.

Hurriedly checking my sextant for index error, I adjusted the arm to an estimated altitude and started peering through the instrument for the sun. I found it, screwed it down to the horizon and took a quick look at my watch.

I had just taken my first sight at sea under "real" conditions. Short on confidence and long on desire for an accurate fix, I took two more sights and then went below to work out lines of position. I hoped fervently that they would plot close together and thus assure me that I had not goofed in some way.

The sights worked out to within a few miles of each other, and in three hours I had a noon shot to go with them for my first good fix at sea.

I was hooked; within ten days, I had made my first landfall off the Island of Maui only four miles from my predicted position. I have stayed hooked ever since, and now want to share my affliction with you.

Any kind of boating can be fun, racing around the marks, or coastwise cruising where there is almost always at hand visual reference ashore from which bearings can be taken for locating one's position and thus finding one's way home. Severing these ties with land, however, offers a new kind of fun, a new kind of freedom, a freedom from dependence on land and the opening of new doors to the world of recreation.

It's a nice, warm, satisfying feeling, I assure you. Your first celestial fix at sea out of sight of land, your first landfall after a trip "out there," will become, like mine, happy, lasting memories.

If you can read, add and subtract, read and understand angles and use a protractor, you can learn to find your position at sea from the heavenly bodies.

That's not much to ask, now, is it?

I. WHAT YOU WILL NEED

Following is a list of materials needed before you begin.

Pencils, a Sharpener and Paper. Later I will propose and offer specific work sheets for particular jobs, but for now, and even out there on the briny, you'll need scratch paper.

A Dependable Timepiece. While you're beginning, at home or around the waterfront, your wrist or pocket watch will do, or even the kitchen clock if it has a second hand and will keep time, and if you can carry it with you when you take your sights. Most cities in the U.S.A. provide reasonably accurate time via the telephone. You can use this for finding watch error while learning.

The following materials will be needed at sea.

A Short-wave Radio. This must be capable of picking up time signals which are broadcast all over the world on a number of wave lengths. "Radio Navigational Aids," H.O. Pubs. Nos. 117-A and 117-B list all time signals, together with their hours of transmission, system used, frequency, and other useful information. I get mine, in the Pacific, on 2.5, 5, 10, 15 and 20 megahertz via WWVH. In the Atlantic it comes via WWV on 2.5, 5, 10, 15, 20 and 25 megahertz. By the way, if you have trouble with reception, try adding a bit of wire to the antenna. It may help.

A Sextant. To do the job accurately you will need a good instrument. This will cost you, at a minimum, around $200. If you want to go first class and can afford it, you can get the best for up to $600. Accuracy, at best, in a small boat at sea is questionable. If you come within a few miles under other than ideal conditions you are doing fine, so I would save my money for something else I need and be satisfied with a $200 yachtsman's model. I use a "baby" model built in Japan (about two-thirds normal size) and I get perfectly satisfactory results. It is a precision instrument with a four-power scope and sells for about $180.

Although my own navigation instructor would be shocked with my next suggestion, I'll make it anyway because my experience at sea proved it useful.

There is on the market a simple plastic sextant that can be purchased for under $15. It is available at most major marine stores. It is barely more than a toy, but, using one on a recent trip from Los Angeles to Honolulu as a second sextant, I found my lines of position falling exactly with those obtained by use of my good sextant. It has no scope and cannot be read without interpolation to closer than two miles. It is, however, in my opinion, an instrument suitable for learning and will make it possible for the student to delay buying the expensive model until he has become proficient and is thus better able to judge whether he wants to go all the way for a first-class sextant.

1

The plastic toy will also continue to be useful as a second sextant to take on deck during those times when merely staying on deck is a feat worthy of note, and one does not want to risk damaging his good sextant. Furthermore, a precise fix on a long passage through open water is not all that important. The plastic sextant can thus save wear and tear on the good one until landfall is expected, or for some other reason a better fix is desired.

The Nautical Almanac for the Current Year. The *Nautical Almanac* can be obtained from most marine stores that deal in navigational equipment, or from The Superintendent of Documents, U.S. Government Printing Office, Washington, D.C., 20402.

Tables of Computed Altitude and Azimuth. Such tables will be available from the same place you purchased your sextant. If not, the dealer can tell you where to find them. There are a number of such publications available, but this book will deal with the set known as *H.O. 249.* These tables are designed for air navigation, but because of their simplicity they are being used by more and more amateur navigators at sea. They are not quite as precise as *H.O.214* (which is being phased out), or the new *H.O. 229* tables, but they provide all the precision you are likely to get in a small boat and are easier to work with. You will need Volume I for star sights, and Volume II for solar system sights between latitudes 0 and 39 degrees either north or south. If you intend to cruise beyond latitude 39, you will need Volume III.

Suitable Charts. These should cover all the waters in which you intend to cruise—large-scale charts for the entire area and detail charts of the harbors where you intend to make landfall. These will also be available where you purchased your other materials. For this learning process I would suggest at least one chart of your general area on a scale of 1:600,000, and another one of just the small area where you will go to take your sights while learning.

Parallel Rulers. These you will need for transferring lines of position and bearings from one place to another on your chart, and for comparing course lines with the compass rose. (More about this later.)

Dividers. Get a good pair; one that will hold its spread when set for stepping off distances.

Protractor. I have two or three "dime-store" models that do a perfectly satisfactory job.

Plot Sheets. You will need a supply of these, but don't worry about it now. When the time comes I will show you a sample and how to make your own.

Work Sheets. These are sheets on which to compute your sights. They constitute a handy reminder of the steps you will take from sight to line of position. I'll have a sample for you when you are ready for it that you can have copied, or make your own.

Now, take a breather, go out and get your tools and materials and we will proceed with the job of learning.

II. LANGUAGE

In celestial navigation, as in other fields of specialized endeavor, there is a vocabulary of words and terms peculiar to the field that must be learned in order to understand the documents and concepts with which you will be working. I will treat the basic ones here, and others as they occur later in the text.

Latitude and Longitude

If you now have a desire to learn celestial navigation, you no doubt already understand this, but for the sake of foundation let us review it briefly.

In order to locate a particular spot on the surface of the earth, the surface is divided into an imaginary grid of lines, some running north and south, and some running east and west. Let us look at a simple grid (Fig. 1). The vertical lines in this example are labeled 1 through 5 and the horizontal lines A through E.

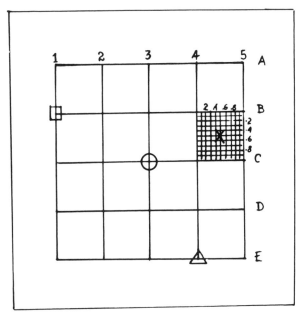

Figure 1

On this grid we can locate the square by the coordinates 1-B. The circle is at 3-C and the triangle at 4-E. To locate the X we will have to divide the grid into finer segments. For this example we will divide each into ten smaller segments and number the lines .1 through .9. Now we can locate the X by the coordinates 4.5 and B.5.

3

The imaginary grid over the surface of the earth becomes an actual grid on the surface of a chart. The vertical lines are labeled longitude, and the horizontal lines latitude.

How Latitude Is Plotted. If we will visualize the earth as an orange hanging in space from its stem end with its blossom end down, and we call the upper end north, then the lower end will be south. Now, if we slice the orange in half crosswise exactly midway between north and south, we will have sliced it at its equator. On the earth this center line that would be represented by the slice is also the equator, or 0 degrees latitude.

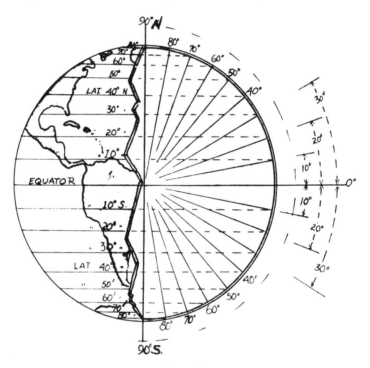

Figure 2

If we then locate the very center of the orange (or the earth) and, with a protractor, measure from there upwards at an angle of ten degrees to the surface and cut the orange again at this point parallel to the equator, we have sliced at ten degrees north latitude. If we measured downwards in the same way, we would be marking ten degrees south latitude.

We could measure and mark in this way for each degree of latitude up to 90 degrees, except for the 90th degree. The 90th degree would merely be points at the top and bottom of the orange, or on the earth, the north and south poles (Fig. 2).

As the earth is round (approximately) like a ball, it can be seen that each degree of latitude is going to be the same distance from its neighboring degree all the way from the equator to the pole. The earth is actually not a perfectly round ball. It has some minor imperfections in it, but for our purposes we can ignore them. For navigational purposes, then, we can consider the distance from one degree of latitude to the next degree to be 60 nautical miles. This is quite a large distance for locating particular spots on the surface, so each degree is divided into 60 subunits called minutes (one minute of arc). A minute, then, is equal to one nautical mile. Surveyors and others who need finer measurements divide the minute into 60 further sub-segments and these are seconds. Each second of arc is equal to 100 feet. For navigation, we will divide the minute into only ten parts and find our finest latitude by degrees, minutes and tenths of minutes. From this we can calculate to the nearest 600 feet, and we should be able to make a proper landfall from this distance.

How Longitude Is Plotted. Longitude is laid out quite differently from latitude, and here again the orange provides a good example.

Figure 3

If we peel our orange and take a good look at the lines that separate the segments of the fruit, we will see that all the lines start at one point at the stem end, run directly down around the fruit and meet again at the other end. The lines are furthest apart at the equator. Longitude lines on the surface of the earth run in exactly the same way.

If we cut the orange at the equator again, we will see that the lines separating the segments come together in the center much like pieces of pie in a pie pan after the pie has been cut. If we were to run a line from the center to the outer edge of the pie and cut it, and then measure ten degrees from the first cut and cut again at that point, we would have a piece of pie ten degrees wide. Longitude lines are measured in this manner. There are 360 degrees in a circle; therefore, there are 360 degrees of longitude all the way around the earth at the equator, or at any other degree of latitude except at the one point of 90 degrees north or south. The degrees of longitude, however, are numbered only up to 180 (or 179). The numbers start at zero and run both east and west from there. The 180th degree is neither east nor west (Fig. 4).

It was a simple matter dividing latitude at midpoint between north and south, but it is not so simple finding a zero point for longitude. Throughout history different points have been used by different people. At this time, however, everyone has pretty much agreed on a starting place. The imaginary line running from pole to pole through Greenwich, England, is the prime meridian, or zero degree longitude. East of Greenwich up to 179 degrees is

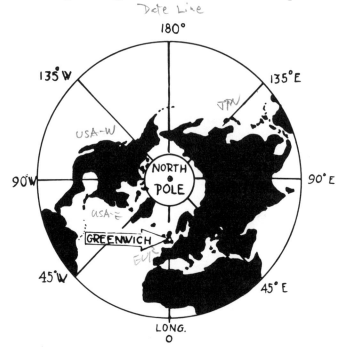

Figure 4

east longitude; west of that point up to 179 degrees is west longitude. The 180th degree is the internationally accepted Date Line where Sunday becomes Monday when crossing from west to east, and Monday becomes Sunday when recrossing.

With all degrees of longitude starting together at the pole, spreading apart toward the equator, and then coming together again at the other pole, it is obvious that one degree of longitude cannot be equal to 60 nautical miles all over the globe. One degree does equal approximately 60 nautical miles at the equator, but the distance decreases from there to nothing at the poles. This is important to remember in navigation as explained in the following paragraph.

A chart is a flat surface which attempts to depict a portion of the earth's surface which is not flat, but round like a part of a ball. All charts have some error, therefore. Coast and Geodetic Survey charts used for most ocean navigation are made by what is called the "Mercator Projection" method. In this method, lines of longitude are drawn parallel to each other and thus the distance between them represents an increasingly lesser distance as one moves from the equator toward the poles. To compensate for this and to keep the relationship between latitude and longitude relatively constant, latitude lines are expanded and drawn further and further apart as one moves toward the poles. Thus: *When reading mileage from the chart, measure the minutes of latitude (miles) from the side of the chart at the latitude where mileage is being measured.* If a long distance north and south is being measured, a measurement at the mid-latitude will average out accurately.

There is a great deal more that can be learned about charts and the information they contain. At this point let me suggest that if you really want to be a student of this and the whole subject of navigation, you should buy a copy of H.O. Pub. No. 9, *American Practical Navigator*, commonly referred to as *Bowditch*. This is published by the U.S. Navy Hydrographic Office and constitutes a complete educational text on everything related to navigation.

Declination (Dec.) and Greenwich Hour Angle (GHA)

If you could project the lines of latitude and longitude straight out into the sky from the surface of the earth, they would be closely related to Dec. and GHA. Let us look at Declination first.

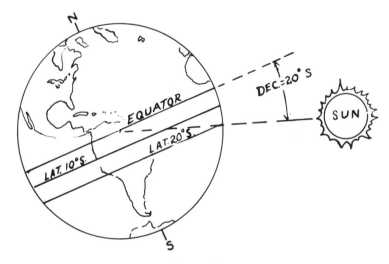

Figure 5

Declination relates to the location of a heavenly body in the sky just as latitude relates to locating a point on earth. For example, if the Sun at a particular moment is directly overhead at latitude 20 degrees south, the declination of the Sun at that moment is 20 degrees south (Fig. 5). Put another way, a string from the center of the earth stretched to the center of the Sun would pass through the surface of the earth at Lat. 20°S. We will sometimes refer to this point on the surface of the earth directly under the body as the Geographical Position (GP) of the body. All heavenly bodies can be located on one coordinate in this manner. Declination is stated in degrees, minutes and tenths of minutes just as is latitude.

We now have one set of imaginary lines in the sky to start our grid for locating heavenly bodies. Now let us consider the other.

Greenwich Hour Angle (GHA) will complete our grid and will correspond with longitude. There is, however, one important difference. Whereas longi-tude is measured from 0 degrees to 180 degrees both east and west from Greenwich, GHA is measured only westward from Greenwich all the way around the earth from 0 degrees to 360 degrees, or back to 0 again.

As the turning of the earth on its axis causes the Sun to appear to rise in the east, move toward and set in the west, GHA is measured, as was men-tioned, toward the west. Thus, when the GHA of a body is 180 degrees or less, GHA and the longitude of the GP of the body are the same. That is, when the Sun is at GHA 10 degrees, it is directly over the 10th longitude west. After the GP passes the 180th degree of longitude, then longitude becomes a decreasing number while GHA continues to increase. This requires a conversion formula when relating GHA to longitude in the eastern hemi-sphere. The formula can be stated as follows: East Long. = 360° - GHA. Let's take a simple example: Assume that GHA is just ten degrees beyond the date line of 180°. GHA would be 190 degrees: 360° - 190° = 170°. For our purposes, then, GHA is the distance westward from Greenwich of the heavenly body in degrees, minutes and tenths of minutes.

Local Hour Angle (LHA)

When measuring the GHA, we are starting at Greenwich as the zero point and measuring westward. Now, if we start at our own position, either esti-mated or actual, as the zero point and measure westward to the GHA of the body, we will be measuring the Local Hour Angle (LHA) of the body. This is a figure we will be using a great deal in celestial navigation. We will be

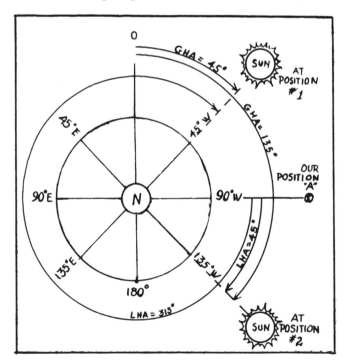

Figure 6

measuring from our assumed position, which will not necessarily be our dead-reckoned position. This is discussed later.

LHA, like GHA, measures all the way around the globe from our position of zero to 360 degrees, or back to zero again (Fig. 6).

In Fig. 6, our position "A" is at 90° W. Long.; with the Sun at position No. 1, GHA 45°, our LHA is 315 degrees. With the Sun at position No. 2, it has passed us and LHA started numbering over again. In this instance, the GHA is 135° and the LHA is 45°. Let us look at another example when our position is in the eastern hemisphere, then we will talk about a formula for determining LHA (Fig. 7).

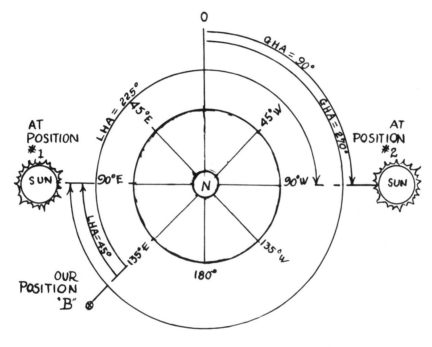

Figure 7

Now, our position "B" is 135° E. Long., and with the Sun at position No. 1, our LHA is 45°. With the Sun at position No. 2 we have an LHA of 225°.

The formula for arriving at LHA can be stated as follows:

$$\text{LHA} = \text{GHA} \quad \begin{array}{l} + \text{ East} \\ \text{Longitude} \\ - \text{ West} \end{array}$$

Let us work a couple of those problems to see how the formula applies. First let's go back to Fig. 6 where our position is in the western hemisphere. With the Sun in its first position we have a GHA of 45°. The formula says "-west" and this refers to our position which is at 90° west. Here's what we have:

$$\begin{array}{lll} \text{GHA} & = & 45° \\ \text{Position} & = & -\ 90° \end{array}$$

Since we are unable to subtract 90 from 45, we add a complete circle (360°) to the 45° thus:

GHA   =   405°
Position = -   90°
LHA   =   315°

Now let's look at Fig. 7 where our position is in the eastern hemisphere. In this case the formula says: " + east". Again, with the Sun in the No. 1 position, we have:

GHA   =   270°
Position = +   135°
LHA   =   405°

In this case, our answer exceeds 360°, so we subtract 360 for an LHA of 45°.

There is a little more to this formula having to do with the treatment of minutes of GHA, but I will explain this when we do our first problem as there are other points you will need to know first.

Greenwich Mean Time

Local time, the time where you are, is generally fixed by time zones, but it may be changed arbitrarily to "save daylight" or for other reasons. For navigational purposes we must have one precise time by which the position of the heavenly bodies can be fixed. With the earth turning 360 degrees in 24 hours it must be obvious that the GHA of an object in the heavens changes rather rapidly. If the heavenly bodies were absolutely stationary in relation to the earth, GHA would change exactly as fast as the earth turns. Actually, none of our relationships with these bodies are positively fixed. They are changing constantly to some extent. This is one reason we need a new *Almanac* each year. Some heavenly bodies, like the stars, change slowly; others, like the planets, change more rapidly. The point at the moment, however, is the importance of accurate and constant time.

To keep our time constant, it must be computed from one specific place on the surface of the earth. That place is again Greenwich, England, thus, Greenwich Mean Time. The navigational day starts at 00: hours, midnight, in Greenwich, England (along the prime meridian—0° Long.), when the "mean" Sun passes over the 180th longitude, the "date line." I stress the word "mean," because the earth does not speed in its orbit around the Sun at a constant rate all year long, thus causing a variation in the time from noon to noon as measured by the Sun's passage overhead. If the actual time of passage over the date line were used, time would not be constant. The fluctuations in this speed have been averaged out to give us mean time to correspond to the average length of a day.

Your *Nautical Almanac*, on the daily pages, lists the 24 hours of the day and gives you the GHA and Dec. for the Sun, Moon, each of the planets suitable for navigation, and the GHA of Aries. You'll learn about Aries later. This time is GMT and it is given on a 24-hour scale.

In the back of the *Almanac*, on colored pages, is a section which will give the change in GHA and Dec. for each minute and second of time. Using the *Almanac*, then, we can find the exact position, GHA and Dec., of a body as of the time we take our sight.

To stress the importance of accurate time, let us take a closer look at the speed of change in GHA.

The GHA of the Sun moves around the earth, 360 degrees, in 24 hours. Dividing 360 by 24 we get a rate of change of 15 degrees per hour. One degree equals 60 nautical miles. Therefore, 60 nautical miles times 15 degrees equals a speed of 900 miles per hour. Dividing further, we'll find that this equals 15 miles per minute or one mile in four seconds. We will be fixing our position by a body moving this fast so it is important to have the exact time for our sights.

Sidereal Hour Angle (SHA)

Volume I, H.O. 249 dealing with stars does not require the use of Sidereal Hour Angle. It does, however, deal only with a selected list of stars with seven of them available at one time. If one desires to use stars which are not listed, he must understand SHA. Whereas your *Almanac* gives the GHA of the bodies in the solar system on each daily page, the stars are listed for three days at a time on each page by SHA. SHA is a system of measuring 360 degrees around the sky over the earth with a beginning, or zero point at the first point of Aries, or at an imaginary line in the sky opposite the point where the Sun is over the equator for the first time during the year (Fig. 8). The GHA of this first point of Aries is given on the daily pages of the *Almanac*, and the minutes and seconds in the minute section, just as for bodies in the solar system. You can find the GHA of a star by looking up the SHA and applying this formula: GHA Aries + SHA star = GHA star. If this number exceeds 360, then 360 is subtracted. While we have Fig. 8 at hand,

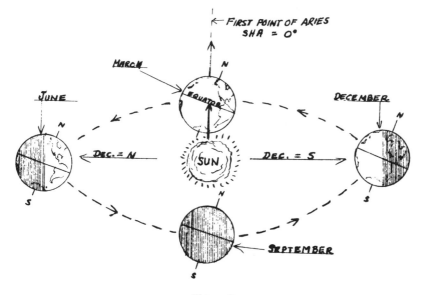

Figure 8

let's discuss stars a little more to give you a better understanding of their use in navigation.

The earth, besides rotating on its axis every 24 hours, swings in its orbit around the Sun once each year. You will note in Fig. 8 that the north-south axis of the earth is not at right angles to the plane of its orbit around the Sun. The North Pole leans away from the Sun at the December position, and toward it at the June position. This results in the Sun having a south Dec. during the September-March period, and a north Dec. during the March-September period. It is during March that the Dec. of the Sun crosses the equator for the first time during the year, thus marking Aries.

A chart in the back of the *Almanac* will show you the location of the navigational stars by SHA and Dec.

There is another phenomenon to note while examining Fig. 8. You will see that at the December position in its orbit, the earth is dark on its half away from the Sun toward the right side of the page. In its June position, the left-hand side is away from the Sun. As we see stars only at night, the sky in June is completely different from the December sky. This change, of course, takes place gradually as the Sun moves around in its orbit. The effect is that the stars rise in the east approximately four minutes earlier each evening.

Altitude (Alt.)

In navigation this is the angular distance (in degrees, minutes and tenths) that a celestial body is above the horizon as measured by the sextant (Fig. 9).

Zenith

This is the point directly overhead (Fig. 9).

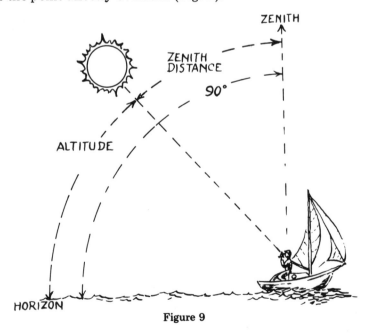

Figure 9

Zenith Distance (ZD)

This is the angular distance from the celestial body to the zenith (Fig. 9).

Azimuth (Zn)

This is the angular distance from north to any other direction (or bearing). It is measured from 0 degrees (north) clockwise around 360 degrees. *H.O. 249, Vols. II* and *III* will give you direction toward the ground spot of an object by Azimuth Angle (Z). This is a bearing measurement from the North Pole which must be corrected to correspond to compass bearing. There is a formula on every page in the tables for converting Z to ZN. We'll take this up further when we get to plotting positions.

true bearing plot

III. TAKING A SIGHT

Taking a sight constitutes measuring the altitude above the horizon of a celestial body with the sextant. Let's take a closer look at the sextant (Fig. 10).

The numbered parts are as follows:

1. On your "good" sextant this will be a small telescope. Some instruments have several scopes that are interchangeable for different uses. On the $15 model this will just be a tubular eyepiece through which you look.

2. Horizon glass. A mirror is on the right side and clear glass on the left. (In some sextants the left side is merely open space.)

3. Index mirror. This is mounted on the index arm directly over the pivot point of the arm.

4. Index arm. A movable arm that pivots at the index mirror at its upper end and swings along the arc at its lower end.

5. Arc. The curved lower member attached to the frame with markings in degrees along its length.

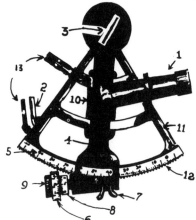

6. Micrometer drum. This is on your good sextant. It is attached to a screw which fits into teeth in the bottom of the frame. One complete turn of the screw will move the arc one degree; a part turn, therefore, will measure minutes of arc.

7. Release. This allows the index arm to be moved freely by disengaging the screw.

8. Vernier for measuring tenths of minutes. The inexpensive sextant will have a vernier instead of a micrometer drum (Fig. 11).

9. Knob, for turning screw.
10. Handle.
11. Frame.
12. Teeth for screw.
13. Sunshades or filters.

Figure 10

In learning to use the sextant, let us start on dry land somewhere around the waterfront where we can get a clear view of the Sun over the ocean. When you find your place, locate it as accurately as you can by latitude and longitude on your chart of the area. In this way you can tell how your lines of position are falling when you take your sights from there.

Altitude Corrections

The sextant, like the compass, does not tell the whole truth at one glance. A number of corrections are required before you have an altitude you can work with. Let us have a look at them.

14

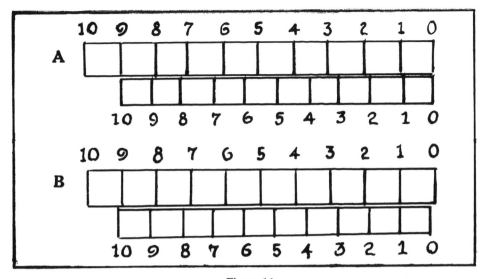

Figure 11

In Fig. 11A and B, the upper and lower scales have been divided into ten segments numbered the same. The divisions in the lower scale are 9/10 the size of the divisions in the upper scale, thus the lower scale is exactly one upper segment shorter than the upper scale.

In Fig. 11A, the lower is aligned with the upper at the zero end of the scale, thus, only the zero and the ten in the lower aligns with the divisions in the upper.

In Fig. 11B, the lower scale has been moved 1/10 of an upper segment to the left. Thus, the line marked "1" in the lower aligns with the "1" in the upper measuring 1/10 of an upper segment. If the lower scale were one more tenth to the left, the "2" would line up on both scales. The same would be true for each tenth of an upper segment that the lower scale is moved to the left. In this way subdivisions of the upper scale can be accurately measured. This is the principle of the Vernier scale used to measure minutes on the cheaper sextant, and tenths of minutes on the good sextant.

Instrument Correction (IC)

Let us assume you are at the waterfront holding your sextant by its handle in your right hand. The first thing to do is to check it for index error. To make this check, set the index arm and the drum at zero. Hold the eyepiece to your eye and sight at the horizon. Be sure you are holding the instrument straight up and down. If your sextant is without error the horizon will appear straight and level right across both the clear part of your horizon glass and the mirror. If the horizon does not line up perfectly, turn the adjustment knob until it does. Handle the knob with the fingers of your left hand.

Even if the horizon does line up, turn the knob until it is out of alignment and then bring it back until it lines up again. Now take a look at the drum and see if you are back to zero. Practice this for a while until you are sure your reading is consistent. Don't worry if you are not coming back to zero each time as long as you come back with a consistent error. The sextant is a delicate tool and its reading may change with changes in temperature or humidity. An error of several minutes is not unusual.

When you have determined the error, record it and indicate if it is a plus (+) reading, (that is, showing a few tenths below zero requiring a correction forward to zero) or a minus (-) reading (showing a bit of altitude which requires a correction back to zero). If the correction is more than a few minutes, take the instrument to a specialist and have it adjusted.

Now, set it at its corrected zero again to realign the horizon. Next, while sighting the horizon, tilt the sextant sidewise first one way and then the other. Tilt it to about 45 degrees and see if the horizon remains aligned. If not, there is lateral error which will require an expert to adjust.

Let's assume that there was no lateral error, but that there was an error of +.3 in the altitude reading. This is the index error and it is corrected with the index correction or IC. This error should be ascertained each time the sextant is used, because, as indicated, it will change from time to time. If the error is a (+) plus it will be added to the reading; if a (-) minus it will be subtracted.

Let's assume an original altitude sight so that we have something to work with as we make our other corrections. Let's say we are "shooting" the Sun at its highest point at noon on May 5, 1972, and we obtain a reading of 85° 00.4'. This is our "Sextant Altitude" and it is referred to as Hs, so we will record it thus:

$$Hs = 85° 00.4$$

We already have one correction, the IC of +.3. This correction is, however, normally combined with the second correction so let's find out about that.

Dip

In taking our sight we are measuring the angular distance between the object (in this case the Sun) and the horizon. We use the horizon because it gives us a reference to a line that is tangent to the surface of the earth.

As the earth is round and not flat, the horizon falls away like the curve in the surface of a big ball. The higher our eye is above the surface the further it falls below a tangent to the surface at the point where we are standing. We must then make a correction for the height of our eye above the surface. This will always be a minus figure as it increases the angle (Fig. 12). The

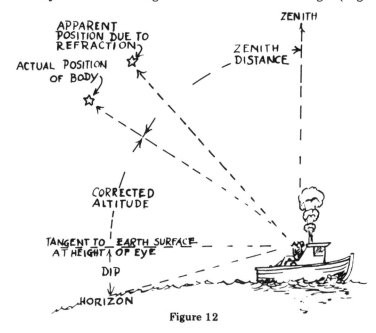

Figure 12

correction for height of eye is called "Dip." Figure 12 includes other corrections besides Dip. We will refer to this figure as these corrections are discussed.

ALTITUDE CORRECTION TABLES 10°-90°—SUN, STARS, PLANETS

Turn now to the inside front cover of your *Almanac*. The *Almanac* format may change from time to time so, if your *Almanac* is different from my 1972 edition, find the page headed "ALTITUDE CORRECTION TABLES 10°-90°—SUN, STARS, PLANETS."

Figure 13 is a duplicate of the portion of the inside front cover of the *Nautical Almanac* dealing with height of eye and the Dip correction. (Note columns for both feet and meters.)

Let's assume that in taking my sight I estimated the height of my eye above the surface of the water at 12 feet. In the column to the right in this illustration I have circled the height of eye figures spanning 12 feet. Under correction (Corr.) I read the figure "-3.4." This is 3.4 minutes as indicated by the minute symbol at the top of the column.

Now, combining this with my IC of +.3 I have a correction of -3.1. I record this as follows:

$$Hs = 85° \ 00.4'$$
$$IC \ and \ Dip = - \ 03.1$$
$$App. \ Alt. = 84° \ 57.3$$

Note, I have introduced a new term. App. Alt. means Apparent Altitude, which is Sextant Altitude corrected for index error and Dip.

DIP

Ht. of Eye	Corrⁿ	Ht. of Eye	Ht. of Eye	Corrⁿ
m		ft.	m	′
2·4	-2·8	8·0	1·0 – 1·8	
2·6	-2·9	8·6	1·5 – 2·2	
2·8	-3·0	9·2	2·0 – 2·5	
3·0	-3·1	9·8	2·5 – 2·8	
3·2	-3·2	10·5	3·0 – 3·0	
3·4	-3·3	11·2	See table ←	
3·6	-3·4	11·9		
3·8	-3·5	12·6	m ′	
4·0	-3·6	13·3	20 – 7·9	
4·3	-3·7	14·1	22 – 8·3	
4·5	-3·8	14·9	24 – 8·6	
4·7	-3·9	15·7	26 – 9·0	
5·0	-4·0	16·5	28 – 9·3	
5·2	-4·1	17·4		
5·5	-4·2	18·3	30 – 9·6	
5·8	-4·3	19·1	32 – 10·0	
6·1	-4·4	20·1	34 – 10·3	
6·3	-4·5	21·0	36 – 10·6	
6·6	-4·6	22·0	38 – 10·8	
6·9	-4·7	22·9		
7·2	-4·8	23·9	40 – 11·1	
7·5	-4·9	24·9	42 – 11·4	
7·9	-5·0	26·0	44 – 11·7	
8·2	-5·1	27·1	46 – 11·9	
8·5	-5·2	28·1	48 – 12·2	
8·8	-5·3	29·2		
9·2	-5·4	30·4	ft. ′	
9·5	-5·5	31·5	2 – 1·4	
9·9	-5·6	32·7	4 – 1·9	
10·3	-5·7	33·9	6 – 2·4	
10·6	-5·8	35·1	8 – 2·7	
11·0	-5·9	36·3	10 – 3·1	
11·4	-6·0	37·6	See table ←	
11·8	-6·1	38·9		
12·2	-6·2	40·1	ft. ′	
12·6	-6·3	41·5	70 – 8·1	
13·0	-6·4	42·8	75 – 8·4	
13·4	-6·5	44·2	80 – 8·7	
13·8	-6·6	45·5	85 – 8·9	
14·2	-6·7	46·9	90 – 9·2	
14·7	-6·8	48·4	95 – 9·5	
15·1	-6·9	49·8		
15·5	-7·0	51·3	100 – 9·7	
16·0	-7·1	52·8	105 – 9·9	
16·5	-7·2	54·3	110 – 10·2	
16·9	-7·3	55·8	115 – 10·4	
17·4	-7·4	57·4	120 – 10·6	
17·9	-7·5	58·9	125 – 10·8	
18·4		60·5		

Figure 13

OCT.—MAR.	**SUN**	APR.—SEPT.			
App. Alt.	Lower Limb	Upper Limb	App. Alt.	Lower Limb	Upper Limb
9 34	+10·8	−21·5	9 39	+10·6	21·2
9 45	+10·9	21·4	9 51	+10·7	21·1
9 56	+11·0	21·3	10 03	+10·8	21·0
10 08	+11·1	21·2	10 15	+10·9	20·9
10 21	+11·2	21·1	10 27	+11·0	20·8
10 34	+11·3	21·0	10 40	+11·1	20·7
10 47	+11·4	20·9	10 54	+11·2	20·6
11 01	+11·5	20·8	11 08	+11·3	20·5
11 15	+11·6	20·7	11 23	+11·4	20·4
11 30	+11·7	20·6	11 38	+11·5	20·3
11 46	+11·8	20·5	11 54	+11·6	20·2
12 02	+11·9	20·4	12 10	+11·7	20·1
12 19	+12·0	20·3	12 28	+11·8	20·0
12 37	+12·1	20·2	12 46	+11·9	19·9
12 55	+12·2	20·1	13 05	+12·0	19·8
13 14	+12·3	20·0	13 24	+12·1	19·7
13 35	+12·4	19·9	13 45	+12·2	19·6
13 56	+12·5	19·8	14 07	+12·3	19·5
14 18	+12·6	19·7	14 30	+12·4	19·4
14 42	+12·7	19·6	14 54	+12·5	19·3
15 06	+12·8	19·5	15 19	+12·6	19·2
15 32	+12·9	19·4	15 46	+12·7	19·1
15 59	+13·0	19·3	16 14	+12·8	19·0
16 28	+13·1	19·2	16 44	+12·9	18·9
16 59	+13·2	19·1	17 15	+13·0	18·8
17 32	+13·3	19·0	17 48	+13·1	18·7
18 06	+13·4	18·9	18 24	+13·2	18·6
18 42	+13·5	18·8	19 01	+13·3	18·5
19 21	+13·6	18·7	19 42	+13·4	18·4
20 03	+13·7	18·6	20 25	+13·5	18·3
20 48	+13·8	18·5	21 11	+13·6	18·2
21 35	+13·9	18·4	22 00	+13·7	18·1
22 26	+14·0	18·3	22 54	+13·8	18·0
23 22	+14·1	18·2	23 51	+13·9	17·9
24 21	+14·2	18·1	24 53	+14·0	17·8
25 26	+14·3	18·0	26 00	+14·1	17·7
26 36	+14·4	17·9	27 13	+14·2	17·6
27 52	+14·5	17·8	28 33	+14·3	17·5
29 15	+14·6	17·7	30 00	+14·4	17·4
30 46	+14·7	17·6	31 35	+14·5	17·3
32 26	+14·8	17·5	33 20	+14·6	17·2
34 17	+14·9	17·4	35 17	+14·7	17·1
36 20	+15·0	17·3	37 26	+14·8	17·0
38 36	+15·1	17·2	39 50	+14·9	16·9
41 08	+15·2	17·1	42 31	+15·0	16·8
43 59	+15·3	17·0	45 31	+15·1	16·7
47 10	+15·4	16·9	48 55	+15·2	16·6
50 46	+15·5	16·8	52 44	+15·3	16·5
54 49	+15·6	16·7	57 02	+15·4	16·4
59 23	+15·7	16·6	61 51	+15·5	16·3
64 30	+15·8	16·5	67 17	+15·6	16·2
70 12	+15·9	16·4	73 16	+15·7	16·1
76 26	+16·0	16·3	79 43	+15·8	16·0
83 05	+16·1	16·2	86 32	+15·8	16·0
90 00			90 00	15·9	15·9

Figure 14

Correction (Corr.) On the left side of the same inside front cover (Fig. 14) is a table which includes a number of corrections. We will simply call it Corr. The major portion of it for the Sun is for semidiameter.

When we take a sight of the Sun we normally bring the bottom edge of the Sun into alignment with the horizon, although we may use the upper edge of the Sun. These two edges are called the lower and upper limbs of the sun. The daily pages in the *Almanac* give the position of the center of the Sun, so we have to make a correction for this "half diameter" no matter which limb we use. Both are included in the Corr. table.

The other major correction included in this one is for refraction. You may remember putting a stick into the water and noting how it appears bent at the surface of the water. This is caused by light refraction. The light is bent as it enters the water. Light behaves in the same way as it enters the atmosphere around the earth. The refraction is different for different angles of entry into the atmosphere. For this reason there are different corrections for different Apparent Altitudes. Please note also that for the Sun there are separate columns for the periods, Apr.—Sept. and Oct.—Mar. The Sun is not at a constant distance from the earth all year long. It is somewhat closer during the Oct.—Mar. period than during the Apr.—Sept. period, thus, it appears larger from Oct.—Mar. and requires a larger correction for semidiameter. Note also that the column we are examining is for Apparent Altitudes 10°-90°. Refraction error increases rapidly with App. Alt. of less than ten degrees, and a separate table is needed for these lower altitudes. These corrections are on the next page facing the inside front cover of the *Almanac*.

There are other small corrections included with this correction, but they are not specifically identified.

The middle section of the inside front cover is headed "STARS AND PLANETS." You will note in your *Almanac* that these corrections are much smaller than for the sun as there is no semidiameter to contend with. There are also listed in this center section, additional corrections for Mars and Venus. We will take these up when we come to them. The Moon corrections are more complex and are located in the back of the *Almanac* in a separate section. We will also take these up when we come to the Moon.

To get on with our problem, we have an App. Alt. so we can find the correction for our sight. I have circled in Fig. 14 the place where I found the correction for our App. Alt. of 84°57.3'. The correction is +15.8'. Our problem now looks like this:

$$
\begin{array}{rcl}
\text{Hs} & = & 85°\ 00.4' \\
\text{IC and Dip} & = & \underline{-\quad 3.1'} \\
\text{App. Alt.} & = & 84°\ 57.3' \\
\text{Corr.} & = & \underline{+\ 15.8'} \\
\text{Ho} & = & 85°\ 13.1'
\end{array}
$$

Note that in adding the minutes of App. Alt. and the Corr., the answer exceeds 60 minutes. Sixty minutes equal one degree, so 60 was subtracted from the minutes, and one degree was added.

I have named the last Altitude, you will note, Ho. This stands for "Observed Altitude" and is, in this instance, the fully corrected Altitude. There could, in some instances, be an additional correction. If you will turn one page in the *Almanac*, you should find a page headed "ALTITUDE CORRECTION TABLES—ADDITIONAL CORRECTIONS." These corrections are for nonstandard conditions of temperature and barometric pressure. You will note upon studying the table that it only applies to Altitudes up to 50° 00'. Instructions at the bottom of the page are complete for application. My sight is well above 50° 00' so the table does not apply. My Ho is the figure I need to compute my sight.

IV. DETERMINING LATITUDE
(The Noon Shot)

The first thing the navigators of long ago learned to do was to determine latitude from the position of the Sun at noon. You may remember from your reading of old sea tales the phrase "running down the latitude" until landfall was made. Latitude could be determined without accurate time by just waiting until the Sun reached its highest point in the sky at noon. Longitude was not easily ascertained until a proper timepiece was developed for use at sea. The navigator would, therefore, take his ship to the latitude of his destination and then run east or west, as the situation warranted, until he arrived.

Today, with the availability of correct time at sea via timepiece or radio, we can obtain an exact latitude and a fair longitude with the one noon sight. This is made possible because we have prefigured information on the Declination and GHA of the Sun at hand in our *Nautical Almanac* as well as accurate time. Let's take a look at the principle involved (Fig. 15).

In this example the Sun is exactly over the equator at Dec. 0°. We are at position A, 30° 00' North (30° 00'N). When the sun reaches its highest altitude in the sky at the hour for noon, our position, it will be due south of us as it passes our longitude. At this point in this example it will be 60° 00' above the horizon. Our ZD would be 30° 00', derived by subtracting 60° 00' from 90° 00'.

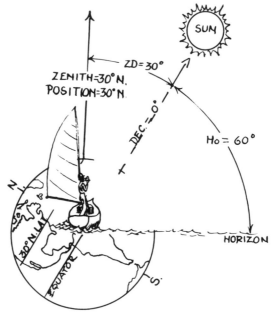

Figure 15

If we were on the equator instead of at 30° 00'N (Fig. 16), the Sun would be 90° 00' above the horizon and our ZD would be 0.

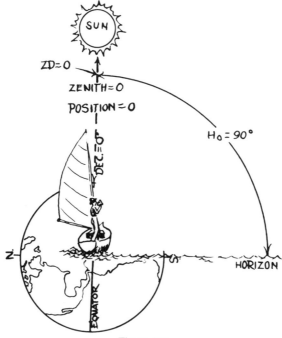

Figure 16

If we were at ten degrees North (10°00'N) the altitude of the Sun would be 80° 00' and the ZD would be 10° 00' (Fig. 17).

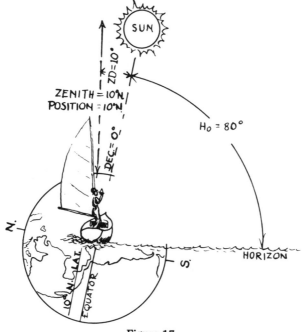

Figure 17

As you can see, if the Sun stayed over the equator, our ZD would equal our latitude. The Sun doesn't stay there, however, so we have to make some simple computations to determine our latitude when the Sun is elsewhere. Let us have a look at another example (Fig. 18).

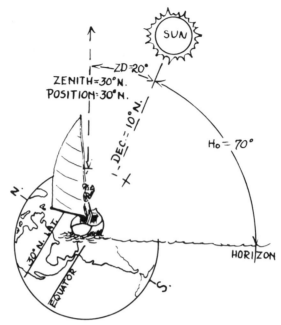

Figure 18

In this example the Sun is at Dec. 10°00′ N and our position is again, 30°00′ N. We are twenty degrees away from the GP of the Sun, so our Ho is 70°00′ and our ZD is 20°00′. If the Sun had been 10°00′ South, we would have been forty degrees away with an altitude of 50°00′ and ZD of 40°00′. This leads to a simple formula for determining latitude. Here it is:

$$\text{Latitude} = 90°00' - \text{Ho} \quad \begin{array}{l} + \text{ same} \\ \\ - \text{ contrary} \end{array} \quad \text{Dec.}$$

As you can see, what we want is our ZD. The formula says, subtract Ho from 90°, and we have it. Then we add Dec. if the Sun is in the same hemisphere as we are, and we subtract it if it is in the contrary hemisphere.

There is one situation, however, when we need a different formula. When the Sun is in our hemisphere, but farther from the equator than we are, we cannot get Lat. by adding Dec. to ZD. The following formula, though, will apply:

When the Sun is poleward in the same hemisphere:

$$90°00' - \text{Ho} = \text{ZD}, \quad \text{Dec.} - \text{ZD} = \text{Lat.}$$

Let us now take a practice noon shot and work it out.

I am in Honolulu and will make my shot from the waterfront at a convenient location. I locate this on the chart at Lat. 21° 17′ N and longitude 157° 52′ W. The date is May 5, 1972. Here on dry land I can figure out from the *Almanac* exactly when the Sun will pass my longitude. At sea, as I will be working from a dead-reckoned position I can figure it out only approximately. Let us learn how to go about it.

You will note that the bulk of the *Almanac* is made up of daily pages with three days on each double page. The year, month, three dates and the days are at the top of each page. Under the top heading on the left-hand page you will find the subheads "Aries, Venus, Mars, Jupiter and Saturn," and then a listing headed "Stars." We will consider these later. What we are interested in now is on the right-hand page. The first subhead there is "Sun" (Fig. 19). Down the left-hand margin you will see the dates and days listed again and immediately to the right of that column of numbers headed with a small "h" for hour. This whole first column is headed at the top of the page, GMT. The columns of figures under the Sun heading are labeled "G.H.A. and Dec." for Greenwich Hour Angle and Declination. The "h" column is for each hour of the day in GMT and what we want to find is the hour before the Sun has passed our longitude. I have found this at the 22nd hour on May 5 and underlined it. The GHA at that time will be 150° 50.9′. The next question is: How far must the Sun travel before it crosses my longitude? I can find that by subtracting its GHA at the 22nd hour from my longitude, thus:

My longitude   = 157° 52.0′
Sun 22nd hour   = 150° 50.9′
                  ‾‾‾‾‾‾‾‾‾‾‾
                   7° 01.1′

Now, what does that mean in time? In the back of the *Almanac* is a section of beige-colored pages with the heading "INCREMENTS AND CORRECTIONS." In the upper corner of each page is a boldface number followed by a small "m." These numbers represent minutes of time. There are four sections on each double page covering four minutes. Down the left-hand margin of each section is a column headed with a small "s." The numbers here are for the 60 seconds in each minute. The left-hand portion of each minute section is headed "Sun—Planets, Aries and Moon." This is the part we are interested in now, so we will ignore the right-hand half of the minute section until later. Under the column headed "Sun—Planets" are columns of figures headed with the symbols for degrees and minutes and the numbers after each second of time on a particular page will tell you how far the Sun (or planet) has moved in GHA during those minutes and seconds of time. We will now thumb slowly through the pages looking for the number nearest the answer to our problem in subtraction. We will find it on the 28-minute page after 4 seconds. The number there is 7° 01.0′, and as the next number down at 5 seconds is 7° 01.3′ we will take the 4-second answer as the closest.

G.M.T.	SUN	
	G.H.A.	Dec.
d h	° '	° '
3 00	180 46·9	N15 38·4
01	195 46·9	39·1
02	210 47·0	39·9
03	225 47·1 ..	40·6
04	240 47·1	41·4
05	255 47·2	42·1
06	270 47·3	N15 42·8
W 07	285 47·3	43·6
E 08	300 47·4	44·3
D 09	315 47·5 ..	45·0
N 10	330 47·5	45·8
E 11	345 47·6	46·5
S 12	0 47·6	N15 47·2
D 13	15 47·7	47·9
A 14	30 47·8	48·7
Y 15	45 47·8 ..	49·4
16	60 47·9	50·1
17	75 48·0	50·9
18	90 48·0	N15 51·6
19	105 48·1	52·3
20	120 48·1	53·0
21	135 48·2 ..	53·8
22	150 48·3	54·5
23	165 48·3	55·2
4 00	180 48·4	N15 56·0
01	195 48·5	56·7
02	210 48·5	57·4
03	225 48·6 ..	58·1
04	240 48·6	58·9
05	255 48·7	15 59·6
06	270 48·8	N16 00·3
07	285 48·8	01·0
T 08	300 48·9	01·7
H 09	315 48·9 ..	02·5
U 10	330 49·0	03·2
R 11	345 49·0	03·9
S 12	0 49·1	N16 04·6
D 13	15 49·2	05·3
A 14	30 49·2	06·1
Y 15	45 49·3 ..	06·8
16	60 49·3	07·5
17	75 49·4	08·2
18	90 49·4	N16 08·9
19	105 49·5	09·7
20	120 49·6	10·4
21	135 49·6 ..	11·1
22	150 49·7	11·8
23	165 49·7	12·5
5 00	180 49·8	N16 13·2
01	195 49·8	13·9
02	210 49·9	14·7
03	225 49·9 ..	15·4
04	240 50·0	16·1
05	255 50·0	16·8
06	270 50·1	N16 17·5
07	285 50·2	18·2
F 08	300 50·2	18·9
R 09	315 50·3 ..	19·6
I 10	330 50·3	20·4
D 11	345 50·4	21·1
A 12	0 50·4	N16 21·8
Y 13	15 50·5	22·5
14	30 50·5	23·2
15	45 50·6 ..	23·9
16	60 50·6	24·6
17	75 50·7	25·3
18	90 50·7	N16 26·0
19	105 50·8	26·7
20	120 50·8	27·4
21	135 50·9 ..	28·1
22	150 50·9	28·8
23	165 51·0	29·5
	S.D. 15·9	d 0·7

Figure 19

What this means is that the Sun will be at our longitude (or at its highest point) at the 22nd hour, the 28th minute and the 4th second GMT on this date. This is our exact noon. This time is also called "Meridian Passage" (MP) as the Sun passes our meridian (Long.) at this time. If we were at sea working from a dead-reckoned position we would start taking sights some 15 minutes before the time, because we would not want to miss the highest point. We would keep changing the altitude until it reached that point, then we would take that as our reading.

While we are in the *Almanac* let us go back to the May 5 page and get our Dec. for the 22nd hour. You will note (Fig. 19) it is: N (North) 16°28.8'. But what do we do about the 28 min. 4 sec. of time? If you will turn back to the 28-minute page you will find out the purpose of the right-hand side of each minute section.

First let us make a check on something on the May 5 page. We found our Dec. for the 22nd hour, but we don't know until we check whether Dec. is increasing or decreasing, so, let's look at the 23rd hour and find out.

The Dec. for the 23rd hour is larger than for the 22nd, so it is increasing. This means that any correction we find, for the minutes and seconds will be added to the Dec. for the 22nd hour.

At the very bottom of the May 5 page under the Dec. column we will find a small "d" and the number 0.7. This is a factor that will help us find the Dec. change we are looking for. The 0.7 is actually the distance of Dec. change in one hour. The minute page will give us the fractional distance for the number of minutes involved. Now examine the 28-min. page (Fig. 20). The three columns to the right are headed "v or d corr." Ours is a "d" but we find them both the same way. There are two columns of numbers under each of three column headings. We will start at the first column and look for 0.7' which we find just a few spaces down. (I have underlined it.) After it we see 0.3', and this is to be added to our Dec. to get Dec. for GMT 22:28:04.

28^m	SUN PLANETS	ARIES	MOON	v or Corr^n d		v or Corr^n d		v or Corr^n d	
s	° ′	° ′	° ′	′	′	′	′	′	′
00	7 00·0	7 01·1	6 40·9	0·0	0·0	6·0	2·9	12·0	5·7
01	7 00·3	7 01·4	6 41·1	0·1	0·0	6·1	2·9	12·1	5·7
02	7 00·5	7 01·7	6 41·3	0·2	0·1	6·2	2·9	12·2	5·8
03	7 00·8	7 01·9	6 41·6	0·3	0·1	6·3	3·0	12·3	5·8
04	7 01·0	7 02·2	6 41·8	0·4	0·2	6·4	3·0	12·4	5·9
05	7 01·3	7 02·4	6 42·1	0·5	0·2	6·5	3·1	12·5	5·9
06	7 01·5	7 02·7	6 42·3	0·6	0·3	6·6	3·1	12·6	6·0
07	7 01·8	7 02·9	6 42·5	0·7	0·3	6·7	3·2	12·7	6·0
08	7 02·0	7 03·2	6 42·8	0·8	0·4	6·8	3·2	12·8	6·1
09	7 02·3	7 03·4	6 43·0	0·9	0·4	6·9	3·3	12·9	6·1
10	7 02·5	7 03·7	6 43·3	1·0	0·5	7·0	3·3	13·0	6·2
11	7 02·8	7 03·9	6 43·5	1·1	0·5	7·1	3·4	13·1	6·2
12	7 03·0	7 04·2	6 43·7	1·2	0·6	7·2	3·4	13·2	6·3
13	7 03·3	7 04·4	6 44·0	1·3	0·6	7·3	3·5	13·3	6·3
14	7 03·5	7 04·7	6 44·2	1·4	0·7	7·4	3·5	13·4	6·4
15	7 03·8	7 04·9	6 44·4	1·5	0·7	7·5	3·6	13·5	6·4
16	7 04·0	7 05·2	6 44·7	1·6	0·8	7·6	3·6	13·6	6·5
17	7 04·3	7 05·4	6 44·9	1·7	0·8	7·7	3·7	13·7	6·5
18	7 04·5	7 05·7	6 45·2	1·8	0·9	7·8	3·7	13·8	6·6
19	7 04·8	7 05·9	6 45·4	1·9	0·9	7·9	3·8	13·9	6·6
20	7 05·0	7 06·2	6 45·6	2·0	1·0	8·0	3·8	14·0	6·7
21	7 05·3	7 06·4	6 45·9	2·1	1·0	8·1	3·8	14·1	6·7
22	7 05·5	7 06·7	6 46·1	2·2	1·0	8·2	3·9	14·2	6·7
23	7 05·8	7 06·9	6 46·4	2·3	1·1	8·3	3·9	14·3	6·8
24	7 06·0	7 07·2	6 46·6	2·4	1·1	8·4	4·0	14·4	6·8
25	7 06·3	7 07·4	6 46·8	2·5	1·2	8·5	4·0	14·5	6·9
26	7 06·5	7 07·7	6 47·1	2·6	1·2	8·6	4·1	14·6	6·9
27	7 06·8	7 07·9	6 47·3	2·7	1·3	8·7	4·1	14·7	7·0
28	7 07·0	7 08·2	6 47·5	2·8	1·3	8·8	4·2	14·8	7·0
29	7 07·3	7 08·4	6 47·8	2·9	1·4	8·9	4·2	14·9	7·1
30	7 07·5	7 08·7	6 48·0	3·0	1·4	9·0	4·3	15·0	7·1
31	7 07·8	7 08·9	6 48·3	3·1	1·5	9·1	4·3	15·1	7·2
32	7 08·0	7 09·2	6 48·5	3·2	1·5	9·2	4·4	15·2	7·2
33	7 08·3	7 09·4	6 48·7	3·3	1·6	9·3	4·4	15·3	7·3
34	7 08·5	7 09·7	6 49·0	3·4	1·6	9·4	4·5	15·4	7·3
35	7 08·8	7 09·9	6 49·2	3·5	1·7	9·5	4·5	15·5	7·4
36	7 09·0	7 10·2	6 49·5	3·6	1·7	9·6	4·6	15·6	7·4
37	7 09·3	7 10·4	6 49·7	3·7	1·8	9·7	4·6	15·7	7·5
38	7 09·5	7 10·7	6 49·9	3·8	1·8	9·8	4·7	15·8	7·5
39	7 09·8	7 10·9	6 50·2	3·9	1·9	9·9	4·7	15·9	7·6
40	7 10·0	7 11·2	6 50·4	4·0	1·9	10·0	4·8	16·0	7·6
41	7 10·3	7 11·4	6 50·6	4·1	1·9	10·1	4·8	16·1	7·6
42	7 10·5	7 11·7	6 50·9	4·2	2·0	10·2	4·8	16·2	7·7
43	7 10·8	7 11·9	6 51·1	4·3	2·0	10·3	4·9	16·3	7·7
44	7 11·0	7 12·2	6 51·4	4·4	2·1	10·4	4·9	16·4	7·8
45	7 11·3	7 12·4	6 51·6	4·5	2·1	10·5	5·0	16·5	7·8
46	7 11·5	7 12·7	6 51·8	4·6	2·2	10·6	5·0	16·6	7·9
47	7 11·8	7 12·9	6 52·1	4·7	2·2	10·7	5·1	16·7	7·9
48	7 12·0	7 13·2	6 52·3	4·8	2·3	10·8	5·1	16·8	8·0
49	7 12·3	7 13·4	6 52·6	4·9	2·3	10·9	5·2	16·9	8·0
50	7 12·5	7 13·7	6 52·8	5·0	2·4	11·0	5·2	17·0	8·1
51	7 12·8	7 13·9	6 53·0	5·1	2·4	11·1	5·3	17·1	8·1
52	7 13·0	7 14·2	6 53·3	5·2	2·5	11·2	5·3	17·2	8·2
53	7 13·3	7 14·4	6 53·5	5·3	2·5	11·3	5·4	17·3	8·2
54	7 13·5	7 14·7	6 53·8	5·4	2·6	11·4	5·4	17·4	8·3
55	7 13·8	7 14·9	6 54·0	5·5	2·6	11·5	5·5	17·5	8·3
56	7 14·0	7 15·2	6 54·2	5·6	2·7	11·6	5·5	17·6	8·4
57	7 14·3	7 15·4	6 54·5	5·7	2·7	11·7	5·6	17·7	8·4
58	7 14·5	7 15·7	6 54·7	5·8	2·8	11·8	5·6	17·8	8·5
59	7 14·8	7 15·9	6 54·9	5·9	2·8	11·9	5·7	17·9	8·5
60	7 15·0	7 16·2	6 55·2	6·0	2·9	12·0	5·7	18·0	8·6

We now have a problem that looks like this:

$$\text{Time of noon} = 22\!:\!28\!:\!04$$
$$\text{Dec. h} = 16°\,28.8'$$
$$\text{m s} = +\ 0.3'$$
$$\text{Noon Dec.} = 16°\,29.1'$$

I am all set for my noon sight now, except for one thing. I need to know what the 22nd hour is in Hawaiian time. As indicated earlier, the format of the *Almanac* may change from time to time, but any year it should have a section in the back on standard and local times. In my 1972 *Almanac* the section is headed "STANDARD TIMES" and is located beginning at page 262. There are three lists of places: LIST I: Places fast on GMT; LIST II: Places keeping GMT; and LIST III: Places slow on GMT. I find Hawaii on List III and it is shown as 10 hours slow. To get my time then, I will subtract ten from 22 and I have my local noon at 12:28:04.

Now, back to the Ala Wai for my sight.

My Latitude is approximately 21 degrees, and the Dec. is approximately 16 degrees, I can therefore estimate the altitude at approximately 85 degrees (16 from 21 = 5; 5 from 90 = 85). I set my sextant to 85 degrees and sight toward the horizon directly under the Sun and there it is sitting just above the horizon. It's a bright day, so I am using the dark filter and the Sun appears as a big green ball. I turn the adjustment knob and the Sun

Figure 20

moves down until the bottom edge is just touching the horizon. At this point I swing the sextant from side to side as though it were a pendulum swinging on a string. The Sun appears to swing as though on a pendulum also, so I note the point where it is at the bottom of the swing. This is the point where my sextant is straight up and down. I do this every time I take a sight and take my reading at the lowest point in the swing (Fig. 21). I note that it is still a few minutes before my time of noon so I wait a minute or two and sight again. This time the Sun has risen from the horizon a bit, so I bring it back down until it is touching again. I keep doing this each minute or so until, just before noon it appears to be motionless in the sky. I leave my sextant at the new setting each time I have to bring it down again, but after it has remained motionless for a few minutes I will notice that it is sinking back into the horizon again. I record the time span that it appeared motionless, and I record the altitude at the highest reading. In this instance its highest point was 85°00.4′. This is the sight I used to illustrate sextant corrections earlier in this text. I corrected it, as you may remember, to an Ho of 85°13.1′.

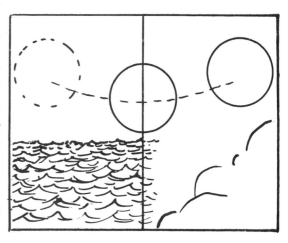

Figure 21

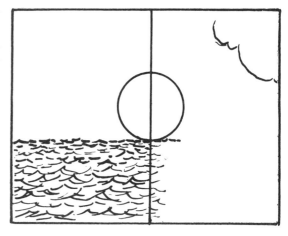

Fig. 22 The Sun as it appears in the horizon glass at the time of my final sight.

Now, to compute my Latitude from this sight. The formula was:

$$\text{Latitude} = 90°00' - \text{Ho} \quad \begin{array}{c} + \text{ same} \\ \\ - \text{ contrary} \end{array} \quad \text{Dec.}$$

When subtracting with degrees, as with hours and minutes, we are only working from a base of ten with the tenths of minutes, therefore when we borrow, except in the minute and tenth columns, we must borrow a full degree of 60 minutes and add these minutes to the minute figure. There are no minutes in 90°00' so we always start this problem by recording 90°00' as 89°60.0'. Then we can subtract our Ho to determine ZD thus:

$$
\begin{array}{rr}
 & 89°60.0' \\
\text{Ho} = & -85°13.1' \\
\text{ZD} = & 4°46.9' \\
\text{Dec.} = & +16°29.1' \\
\text{Latitude} = & 20°76.0'
\end{array}
$$

Dec. is "same" so

There are too many minutes in the answer so we will take away 60 min. and add one degree for a Lat. of 21°16.0'.

To obtain an approximate longitude from this sight, I would note the time span when the Sun appeared stationary, select the midpoint in that time and then look up the GHA of the Sun at that moment. This would be within a few miles of my longitude. If I were in the eastern hemisphere I would have to convert GHA to longitude.

Remember, when at sea working from a DR position, start sighting early enough to be sure you don't miss noon.

Here are two more Latitude problems; run through them until you understand them.

1. Date   12/23/72

    DR   Lat. 21°18.5'N—Long. 157°50.8'W.

    HE   10 feet.   No IC.

    Hs   45°03.9'

What is the latitude? What is the time of noon (Meridian Passage)?

2. Date   6/11/72

    DR   Lat. 21°18.0'N—Long. 157°50.5'W.

    HE   10 feet.   No IC.

    Hs   87°57.6'

What is Latitude? What is time of noon?

Now, if you have finished your problems you will see that latitude shots are simple. You don't need *H.O. 249* and you don't even need to remember the formulas. If you forget the formulas, here is how you can still figure out your latitude:

1. All you have to remember is that your latitude is measured in degrees and minutes from the position (declination) of the Sun as it passes you at noon, either to the south or north. Your distance is the difference between the Ho of the Sun and 90 degrees.

2. In case of doubt about formulas, plot the position of the GP of the Sun on your chart (declination equals latitude) as it passes.

3. Compute your Zenith distance and measure that off on the chart in the direction (north or south) that you were when it passed, and that is your latitude.

4. If you are lost, do as the old-time sailors did; sail to the latitude of your destination and then east or west as the case may be, until landfall.

And finally, if you are the skipper, or the only navigator in the crew, see that everyone aboard knows how to do this one thing at least. The life you save may be your own.

V. LINE OF POSITION (LP)—FIX

Let us assume that we are cruising along an unfamiliar shore searching for the entrance to a small hideaway harbor which we have located on the chart. We cannot see the entrance to the harbor, but we do identify a large water tank inland that we find on the chart. From this tank we can plot a Line of Position (LP) by simply taking a bearing on it with our pelorus. If we have no pelorus, we can simply head the boat toward the tank and read the compass. Let us assume that we do this and the tank bears 43 degrees true from our position. If we then add 180 to the 43 degrees we will obtain a reciprocal, or opposite, bearing from the tank to us. This is a bearing of 223 degrees. We plot this on the chart from the tank and it becomes LP TANK. We are somewhere on this line. This is helpful information, but if we are to plot an accurate course to the harbor we need to know *where* on the line. To find out where, we need a second LP which will cross the first, preferably at an angle close to 90 degrees.

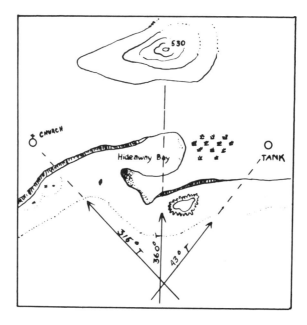

Figure 23

Next, we spot a church steeple in a small village farther along the shore and we are able to locate this on the chart and find it bears 315° from us. We subtract 180° from this and obtain a reciprocal of 135 degrees. We plot this in the same way and obtain a FIX at the point where the two lines cross. From here we can plot a course to the mouth of the harbor in reasonable safety.

28

Navigators are by habit cautious and like to prove their FIXES by taking a third sight when possible, in order to assure that there is no mistake in either of the first two lines of position. In our case, let us assume that we find a mountain peak inland, due north and plot a third line of position from this. Now we have a three-point FIX. You will note in this example (Fig. 23), the lines leave a small triangle at the point where they intersect. A perfect FIX would have all three lines crossing at exactly the same place, but this seldom happens in practice. Remember, the boat is probably moving a little from current or wind even with the engine off or the sails down. Such perfect accuracy is hard to come by except in theory.

A celestial Line of Position, and a celestial FIX is arrived at in very much the same way as in this example, except that celestial bodies are used instead of terrestrial bodies. Our *Nautical Almanac* replaces our chart to tell us where the bodies are at a given moment in time (GHA and Dec.).

A line of position in celestial navigation is actually a small segment of a circle of position. Let me show you how this comes about.

Assume that we are at a position, 23° 00′ North Lat. 140° 00′ West Long. in the Pacific on the way from California to Hawaii. At the moment of our sight the GHA of the Sun is 120° 00′ and the Dec. is 20° 00′ North (all approximate). We would get an altitude of approximately 70° 00′ as the Sun is 20 degrees away from our position. At this same time if there were a ship at 100° 00′ West Long. and at 23° 00′ North Lat., it would also be 20 degrees away from the GP of the Sun and would get the same altitude, although an opposite azimuth. A ship north or south the same distance would also get the same altitude. To put it another way, any ship on a circle of 20 degrees away from the ground spot of the Sun would get the same altitude reading from a sight. Thus, one sight alone results in a circle of position. A boat could be anywhere on the circle 20 degrees away from the Sun and get the same altitude reading. If we take a sight on a second object we can create a second circle of position which will intersect the first in two places. We should know from our DR which intersection represents our position, but a third sight will intersect at only one of the first points and confirm our position. In practice we do not construct a circle, but only a short straight line representing a segment of the circle. The tables give us an azimuth toward the heavenly body and this is sufficient for our purposes. Let's see how it works.

Step by Step to a Line of Position

We will still be using the Sun. It is a big bright ball and easy to find when there are not too many clouds. We can also use it for three different sights at different times and get a pretty good three-point FIX with just this one body, but let us calculate an LP before we get into that.

The steps are:

1. Time is important. Check your timepiece and record the error down to the second. For this example let us say that we have tuned in on 5 megahertz and determined that our watch is 20 seconds fast. We are sailing from California to Hawaii, and our watch is set to Pacific Coast Time. The month is

July. A look at the "Standard Time" section of the *Almanac* will inform us that the Pacific Coast is on Daylight Saving Time during July.

2. Now, up on deck with pencil and paper. (We will work with a work sheet later.) Find a comfortable place where you can brace yourself against the motion of the boat, then check and record IC and Height of Eye.

3. Estimate the altitude of the Sun and set the sextant at that altitude. Select a Sun filter and move it into place. Now, look at the horizon through the scope and see whether the Sun is there near the horizon. If not, release the index arm and move the arm forward and back until you find it. If you still don't see it you are probably not pointing the sextant directly toward the Sun. Look around, it's there somewhere. When you find it, you may want to change the filter. The light should be screened enough so that it is comfortable to look at but still sharp and clear.

4. Take your sight just as you did for the noon shot. Some navigators like to place a morning sun (one that is rising) just below the horizon and wait for it to come up to position. An afternoon shot would be taken by placing the sun just above the horizon and letting it drop into position. I prefer to bring it slightly above, swing my sextant to find the bottom of the arc, and then screw it down until it touches.

5. If you have a helper, he will be holding the watch. You will call, "Ready" and then "Mark" as you bring the lower limb of the sun in tangent with the horizon. I do not generally use a helper. I wear my watch on my left wrist which is right in front of my eye as I adjust the sextant. I estimate that it takes me one second to focus my eyes from the Sun to the watch. I subtract the second from the time that I read. In checking the time, pick up the position of the second hand first, then the minutes and finally the hour. At morning or evening twilight you will be better with a helper to read not only the time, but the sextant as well. A flashlight may be needed for this, and the navigator taking the sight should keep his eyes dark adapted so the stars will be easier to find.

If the sea is rough, or if for any reason you doubt your sight, take two or three during a span of a few minutes and work them all out for an average. If one is obviously bad, throw it out and don't use it.

6. Record the time and the altitude of your shot, or shots and return to the cabin.

Now it is time to introduce the work sheet (Fig. 24). You will note that the upper section is a heading of general information needed as a passage progresses. I have not numbered these lines. Below the heading each line is numbered and we will proceed with our steps from here by the line number on the work sheet. *(Note: Fig. 24 is on page 34.)*

Line 1—I have recorded the DR position; Lat. and Long.

Line 2—This is my IC and HE.

Line 3—The body is the Sun. I use the symbol for the Sun.

Line 4—I record my Hs.

Line 5—My correction for HE and IC.

Line 6—My App. Alt.

Line 7—My correction for the App. Alt.

Line 8—My Ho.

Line 9—The time of my sight by day, hour, minute and second.

Line 10—My watch was 20 seconds fast so my correction for this is -20s.

Line 11—I have converted to GMT from Pacific Coast time and have made my watch correction.

The next section of the work sheet is headed "DECLINATION—FROM THE ALMANAC."

Line 12—In my *Almanac* I find July 11 on page 139. Under the heading "SUN" I find the 17th hour and read the Dec. there as 22°01.9'. I record that on this line.

Line 13—This is the Dec. correction for minutes and seconds of time. I need to know first which way Dec. is changing, so I look at the Dec. for the 18th hour and find that it is smaller, therefore, Dec. is decreasing so I circle the (-) sign on this line and then from the very bottom of the Sun column I pick up and record the code "d" of 0.4. This is a multiplication factor, and it will help me find the Dec. change for 35 min. 47 sec. I will not find the correction until I turn to the minute pages, which I will do after I get my GHA in the next section.

Line 14—This is where I computed final Dec. after I got the correction.

Line 15—In the GHA section of the work sheet I read the GHA after the 17th hour on the July 11 page where I found the Dec. I recorded it here and then turned to the 35 minute page in the back of the *Almanac.*

Line 16—On the 47 sec. line of the 35 min. page I read: 8°56.8'. This is the distance the Sun moved in 35 minutes and 47 seconds. I recorded it here.

Line 17—We will meet the "v" correction to GHA when we get to the Planets and the Moon. It does not apply to the Sun so we leave this line blank and add up our GHA figures.

Line 18—Record the answer here.

Now, while we are on the minute page, look at the right hand half of the 35 minute section and down the v-d corr. column until we find the 0.4 that we recorded on line 13. We find it just the fifth number down in the first column of v-d corrections and after it is our corr. of 0.2. We now record this on line 13, and then subtract it from line 12 for a final Dec. on line 14.

Line 19—This line moves into a new section of the work sheet and, for the moment we are through with the *Almanac.* On this line I have assumed a longitude that has exactly the same minutes as appears in the GHA of the sun. We will compute our LHA from our Assumed Long., and as the Sight Reduction Tables, *(H.O. 249 Vol. II)* are designed for entry in whole degrees of LHA, we must assume a position that will give us whole degrees. If we were in the eastern hemisphere, where as you will remember, longitude **reduces in number as one moves west, while GHA increases, we would assume** a number of minutes which when added to the minutes of GHA would equal sixty. This would give us whole degrees of LHA for the eastern hemisphere. Our next problem will be in the east, so we can see how it works there when we go on.

Line 20—I have recorded my LHA. Do you remember the formula? It goes like this with an added note on minutes:

$$\text{LHA} = \text{GHA} \quad \begin{matrix} + \text{ east} \\ \text{longitude}- \\ - \text{ west} \end{matrix} \quad \begin{matrix} \text{east minutes} = 60 \\ \\ \text{west minutes} = 0 \end{matrix}$$

My problem, then, looked like this:

$$GHA = 82°34.7'$$

Minus west Long. $139°34.7'$

In order to subtract, I must add 360 degrees to the GHA to make it large enough. My problem is now like this:

$$GHA = 442°34.7'$$
$$- 139°34.7'$$
$$LHA = 303°00.0'$$

Line 21—Here again the tables are designed for entry by whole degrees of Lat., so we will assume the nearest whole degree of 25°.

Line 22—Once more the tables must be entered with whole degrees. We will therefore assume the whole degree of Dec. as shown on line 14. We will have to consider the remainder of the Dec. figure, however, so:

Line 23—We will record it here.

We now have all that is necessary for entering the tables, so to *H.O. 249, Vol. II.*

There are three places where I said we would need whole degrees to get into the tables; Lines 20, LHA, 21, Lat. and 22, Dec. We go in first with Lat.

If you will thumb through your *H.O. 249 Vol. II* you will see that the first 12 pages numbered with Roman numerals are introductory pages. Following the introduction you will find pages labeled "LAT." There are several pages for each LAT. Open the book to pages headed with our assumed Lat. of 25°. This Lat. section begins on page 150. If you will thumb ahead you will see that Lat. 25 runs through page 155. Page 153 is the one we want. Turn to it and we will see why. Turn the book sidewise so that the printing is properly oriented and you will see across the top of the page heading: "DECLINATION (15-29) *SAME* NAME AS LATITUDE." We want this page for three reasons. First, our Dec. is 22° and that falls between 15 and 29. Second, if you will look down the far right column headed LHA you will find that our LHA of 303° is there. Third, the word "SAME" is in the title. If you will check the title on page 152 you will see that it is "DECLI-NATION (15-29) *CONTRARY* NAME TO LATITUDE." The "SAME" means that the Dec. of the body we are sighting is in the same hemisphere, north or south, as our latitude. The "CONTRARY" is for a body in the opposite hemisphere. Our position is north, the Sun's Dec. is north, therefore we want the page marked "SAME."

Running across the top of page 153 right under the heading are columns of figures of numbers from 15 to 29. This is for Dec. and as our Dec. is 22° we want that column. Now, look down the right hand column headed LHA until we find our 303. Place a straight edge under 303 to mark it and then look under the Dec. column of 22°. You will find three sets of numbers in that space. Glance at the top of the column and you will see that they are subheaded: Hc, d, and Z. Back down on the 303 LHA line we read under Hc, 38°01'. Under d we read 16, and under Z, 81.

Line 24—We copy these three numbers in the spaces provided for them here.

The Hc figure represents what our Ho would be if we were at Lat. 25° exactly; at an LHA of exactly 303° and if the Dec. were exactly 22°. The "d" is a factor to go with our Dec. remainder to correct for the exact declination. The "Z" will give us a direction toward the GP of the Sun.

Let's go on and work it out.

Line 25—This is for the Dec. correction and I must first see if it is a plus or a minus. You will note that there is a plus (+) or a minus (−) sign with the correction. In this case it is a plus (+) so I mark mine with a + sign on this line. Next, the last page of *H.O. 249* is a table numbered 5. There should be a second copy of this on a card that came with your volume. Table No. 5 has numbers across the top from one through 60. Down each side are numbers from 0 through 59. You have two numbers to work with, your Dec. remainder and the d factor on line 24. The Dec. remainder of 1.7 is closer to 2 than to 1 so we will change it to 2 as the table doesn't handle tenths. Across the top of Table No. 5 we find our d factor of 16. Reading down the side we find 2. In the space where these two coordinates meet we find a correction of 1. This is one minute so we record it on line 25 in the space provided.

Line 26—By adding lines 24, and 25, we have a corrected Hc.

Line 27—This is my Ho which I brought down from line 8.

Line 28—I next compare my Hc and my Ho. I note that my Ho is larger.

It is quite easy to visualize, I think, that when an object in the sky is far away it will appear lower in the sky than when it is near. We learned that this was so with our noon shot. If we are at the GP of the body it will be directly overhead at 90 degrees. The farther away it is, the lower it will be when we measure its altitude.

In comparing our Ho with Hc we make the same kind of a check. In this instance our Ho is larger than Hc, which means that we are closer to the body than if we were at the assumed position. This being so, I circle the T on line 28 to indicate that we are "Toward" the body from our assumed position. If Ho had been smaller, I would have circled the A for "Away" from the assumed position.

Now, I will subtract the smaller from the larger and see how far toward. My answer is on:

Line 28—51 minutes of arc equals 51 miles, therefore, my line of position will be drafted 51 miles toward the GP of the Sun from my assumed position.

Back on line 25 to the right of the corr. is a Zn that needs to be figured out. In *H.O. 249* on page 153 where we found our Hc we can find a formula for converting the Z to a Zn. (Azimuth).

At the top left corner is a formula as follows:

LHA greater than 180° . . . . . Zn = Z

N. Lat.

LHA less than 180° . . . . Zn = 360° − Z

Our LHA is greater, so our Zn is the same as Z, or 81°.

WORK SHEET ---------- SOLAR SYSTEM

DATE _July 11 1972_ MILES RUN LAST POSITION _____

COURSE _240° M_ MILES MADE GOOD _____

LOG _1,195 Mi_ TOTAL MILES RUN _____ MILES TO GO ____

1- DR Lat. _25°28'N_ DR Long. _139°03' W_ COMPUTED: Lat. _____ Long. _____

2- IC _0_ HE _8'_	IC ____ HE ____	IC ____ HE ____
3- Body _☉_	Body ____	Body ____
4- Hs _38° 41.0'_	Hs ____	Hs ____
5- IC & HE _- 2.8'_	IC & HE ____	IC & HE ____
6- App. Alt. _38° 38.2_	App. Alt. ____	App. Alt. ____
7- corr. _+ 14.8'_	corr. ____	corr. ____
8- Ho _38° 53.0_	Ho ____	Ho ____

TIME OF OBSERVATION

9- _11_ d _10_ h _36_ m _07_ s	____ d ____ h ____ m ____ s	____ d ____ h ____ m ____ s
10- watch corr. _- 20_ s	watch corr. ____	watch corr. ____
11- GMT _11_ d _17_ h _35_ m _47_ s	GMT ___ d ___ h ___ m ___ s	GMT ___ d ___ h ___ m ___ s

DECLINATION --- FROM ALMANAC

12- mo.-day-hour _22° 01.9' N_	mo.-day-hour ____	mo.-day-hour ____
13- code d _0.4_ corr ⊕ _0.2_	code d ___ corr.± ___	code d ___ corr.± ___
14- DEC. _22° 01.7'_	DEC. ____	DEC. ____

GHA -----------FROM ALMANAC

15- mo.-day-hour _73° 37.9_	mo.-day-hour ____	mo.-day-hour ____
16- min.-sec. _8 56.8_	min.-sec. ____	min.-sec. ____
17- code v ___ corr± ___	code v ___ corr± ___	code v ___ corr± ___
18- GHA _82° 34.7_	GHA ____	GHA ____
19- Ass. Long. _139° 34.7_	Ass. Long. ____	Ass. Long. ____
20- LHA _303°_	LHA ____	LHA ____
21- Ass. Lat. _25° N_	Ass. Lat. ____	Ass. Lat. ____
22- Ass. Dec. _22° N_	Ass. Dec. ____	Ass. Dec. ____
23- Dec. remainder _01.7'_	Dec. remainder ____	Dec. remainder ____

FROM HO 249

24- Hc _38° 01_ d _16_ z _81_	Hc ____ d ____ z ____	Hc ____ d ____ z ____
25- corr ⊕ _01_ Zn _81°_	corr± ____ Zn ____	corr± ____ Zn ____
26- Hc _38° 02.0_	Hc ____	Hc ____
27- Ho _38° 53.0_	Ho ____	Ho ____
28- _51'_ A or ⊤	A or T	A or T

Figure 24

VI. PLOTTING A LINE OF POSITION (LP)

Let's start by examining Fig. 25. (This plot sheet was designed by Mr. Louis Valier of 2969 Kalakaua Avenue, Honolulu. Louis taught navigation at the Bishop Museum in Honolulu and has sailed his own boat extensively throughout the Pacific over the past many years. The plot sheet has no copyright, and its design is available to you for your use. If you are interested in acquiring a supply I would suggest you write Mr. Valier at the above address. He makes them available in pads at a nominal price.) This is a universal plot sheet designed to use at any latitude, or longitude where a Mercator chart is applicable. In blank form it has one horizontal line through the center and three vertical lines. To make it applicable to the area you are in you will: No. 1, name the center horizontal line your assumed Lat. In our problem this is 25° North. At No. 2, I have named the center vertical my whole degree of assumed longitude, 139°. The minutes of longitude are along the scale at the top and bottom of the sheet. At No. 3, I have named the two adjacent vertical lines to correspond to the proper longitude. In the lower left corner of the sheet is a printed protractor. I have marked lines from the corner of the sheet through the 26th degree at No. 4, and through the 24th degree at No. 5, and have measured the length of these lines with a pair of dividers to give me the distance to Lat. 26° and 24° from Lat. 25°. I have drawn in and labeled these lines. The sheet is now ready for use for our Sun sight.

Now, let us look at Fig. 26. Here I have worked out a line of position (LP).

At No. 1, I have marked in the assumed position. I placed it on Lat. 25°, and then located, as accurately as I could, 34.7 minutes of longitude to the left of Long. 139°. I used the Long. scale at the top and bottom of the sheet for this. I labeled the point "AP" for Assumed Position.

Now, with a protractor I measured off 81°, our Zn, (No. 2) and drew a line from the AP through the point so marked. I put an arrowhead on the end to indicate direction and then the symbol for the Sun.

Back at the work sheet again, on line 28 I picked up 51 mi. "T", or 51 miles toward the Sun from my AP. You will remember when I was discussing latitude and longitude I pointed out that one minute of longitude equaled one nautical mile only at the equator. The scale at the bottom left hand side of the plot sheet running from 0 through 60 would be our mileage scale at the equator. To get the scale for any other latitude, a line is drawn from the left lower corner of the protractor through the degree, equal to the degree of latitude at the AP. Then measurement is made along the sloping line created. Ours is the 25th degree. You will note that subdivisions are drawn in up to 30 minutes only. When the mileage measurement is more than that, it can be measured from the right hand end of the line. This I have done for 51 miles and then transferred the distance to my Zn line toward the Sun. Next, at No. 3, with my protractor, I have drawn in my LP at that point 90 degrees from the Zn line. This is my LP. I am somewhere on it.

You might also note that I have indicated my DR position on the plot sheet.

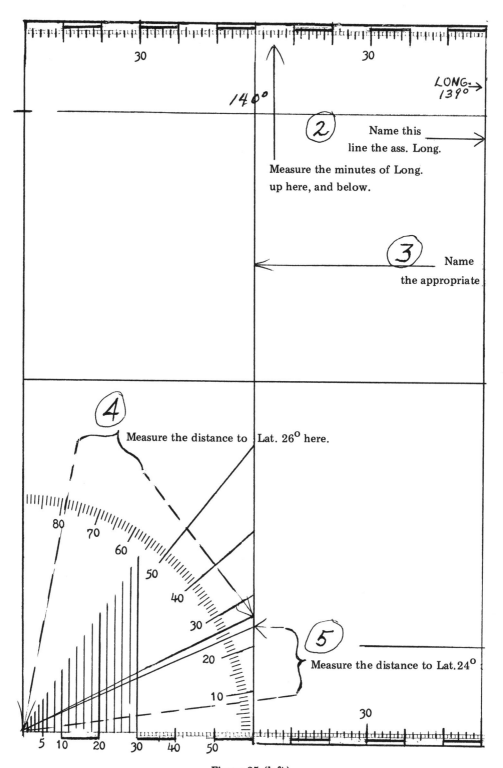

30   30

LONG.→
139°

140°

② Name this
line the ass. Long. →

Measure the minutes of Long.
up here, and below.

③ Name
the appropriate

④ Measure the distance to Lat. 26° here.

80 70 60 50 40 30 20 10

⑤ Measure the distance to Lat. 24°

30

5 10 20 30 40 50

Figure 25 (left)

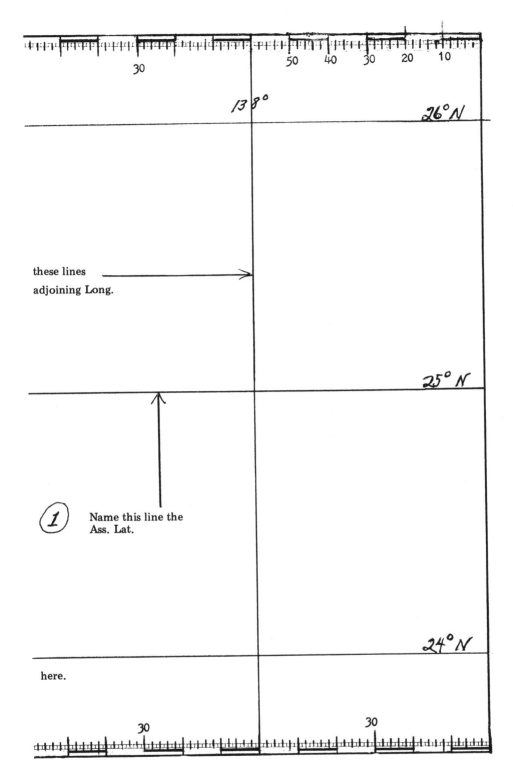

these lines
adjoining Long.

13 8°

26° N

25° N

① Name this line the
Ass. Lat.

24° N

here.

Figure 25 (right)

37

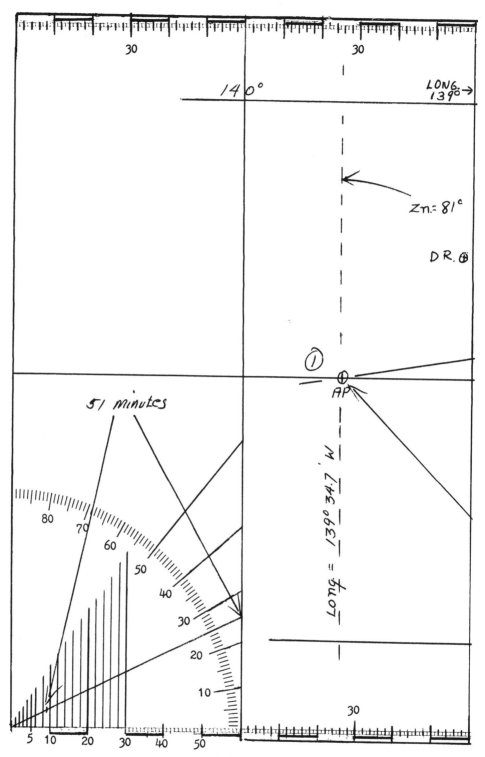

Figure 26 (left)

38

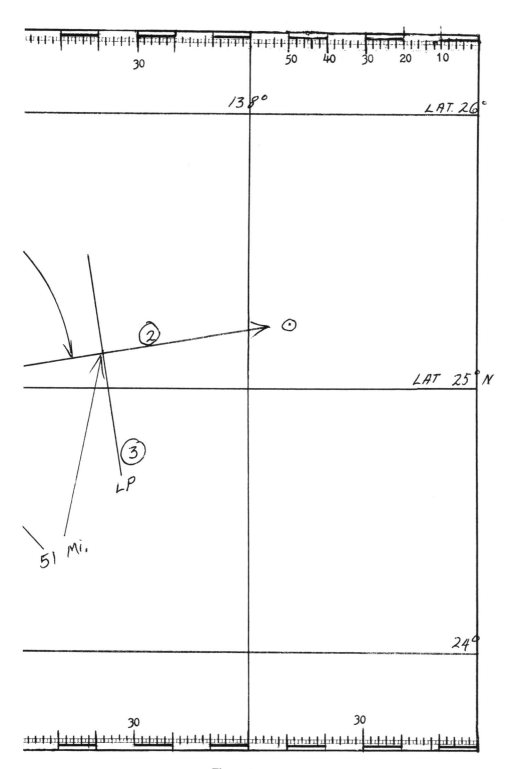

Figure 26 (right)

VII. FIX

Just as a single line of position from a point on shore failed to give us an exact FIX, so does a single line of position from a celestial body. We can, however, gleen some worthwhile information from a single line. As we learned earlier, a single line at noon gives us an accurate latitude. A single line of position when the Sun is astern or ahead will give us a good indication as to how far along our track we are. If we are cruising north or south along a shore, a morning or afternoon LP taken when the Sun is abeam, or near abeam will tell us how far off shore we are. A morning sight giving us an LP running roughly north and south can be crossed with a noon sight for a fairly accurate noon FIX. To obtain this FIX we would move our morning LP in the direction we are cruising, equal to the miles run between the two sights (Fig. 27). This FIX can be further confirmed with an afternoon sight moved back the miles run, for a three point FIX from one body. The FIX will be only as good as the measurement of miles and direction run, but in the open ocean away from danger this is not a bad FIX.

The moon is available for a sight a good part of the time during daylight hours, and a second line can be computed from this to cross with a Sun line. Venus, likewise, can sometimes be seen during daylight and thus can be used with the Sun and the moon.

When we get to stars, there will be an abundance of heavenly bodies to choose from for a three point FIX, but we are not into stars yet so let us get back to the Sun and see what will happen when we are in the eastern and southern hemispheres. We will take both eastern and southern problems with a trip from Australia to the West Coast of the United States.

We are now sailing off the east coast of New Guinea headed for a stopover on New Ireland and have worked out a dead reckoned (DR) position of 4°30'S. Lat. 148°40'E. Long. (Fig. 28). The date is May 15, 1972. You can follow the work sheet from my Hs down through line 8. There are no new problems here. On line 9, the captain, we find is keeping Queensland, Australia time, and he has to convert to GMT. (He'd cure this problem if he kept a watch on GMT.) The sight is taken at 8:15:12 a.m. If you will look up Queensland in the standard time section of the *Almanac* you will find it in List 1 at 10 hrs. early on GMT. Ten hours from the 8th hour of the day takes us back to the previous day at the 22nd hour. GMT then is the 14th of May and this is shown on line 11 of the work sheet.

We next extract Dec. and GHA for that hour, check the direction of Dec. change, and then pick up the d code and turn to the minute page. Note that in adding the minutes of GHA there are 103.6 minutes, so 60 are subtracted and one degree is added.

Now for the LHA problem. I must remember two differences from the first problem in the western hemisphere. 1. I must assume a number of minutes and tenths which will equal 60 when added to GHA rather than using the same number of minutes and tenths. 2. I will then add the assumed

Long. to the GHA to get LHA rather than subtract it. Remember the formula? It is in the early pages of the text and goes thus:

$$LHA = GHA \quad \begin{matrix} - \text{ west} \\ \\ + \text{ east} \end{matrix} \quad \text{longitude.}$$

Here is our problem:

$$
\begin{aligned}
GHA &= \quad 154°43.6' \\
\text{Ass. Long.} &= + \underline{148°16.4'} \\
&\quad \ \ 302°60.0'
\end{aligned}
$$

$$LHA = \quad 303°$$

The problem is then completed just as in the first example.

When making this plot (Fig. 29) note first that Lat. and Long. are numbered in reverse as compared with a plot in the western and northern hemispheres. As for "Z," if you will turn to page 29 in your *H.O. 249 Vol. II* where the Hc, d and Z are located, you will see the formula for converting Z to Zn in the southern hemisphere at the bottom left corner of the page.

It reads thus:

> LHA greater than 180° ..... Zn = 180 – Z
>
> S. Lat.
>
> LHA less than 180° ..... Zn = 180 + Z

In this problem, LHA is greater, so Z is subtracted from 180 for a Zn of 67°.

I hope you haven't been loafing, but if you have, I'll get even with you now.

The next two exhibits, Figs. 30 and 31 are pages from the 1972 *Almanac*. There is a daily page and a minute page. You have four extra spaces on the work sheets used as exhibits up to now. I'll let you use two of those spaces for sights of your own which I want you to take and compute. The other two spaces can be used to solve the following problems.

One: Hs, Lower Limb: 17°40.0'   ☉
    The date is August 20, 1972.
    DR = Lat. 28°10' N., Long. 130°30' W.
    Time = Pacific Coast Daylight Saving, 8:40:10 a.m.
    IC = 0.
    HE = 9 feet.
    The answer is: 7.9 Mi. Away. You work it out to the same answer.

Two: Hs, Lower Limb: 48°34.5'   ☉
    The date is August 21, 1972.
    DR = Lat. 27°00' N., Long. 133°45' W.
    Time = Pacific Coast Daylight Saving, 4:41:50 p.m. (16:41:50).
    IC = 0.
    HE = 12 feet.
    The answer is: 4.2 Mi. Toward. Can you prove it?

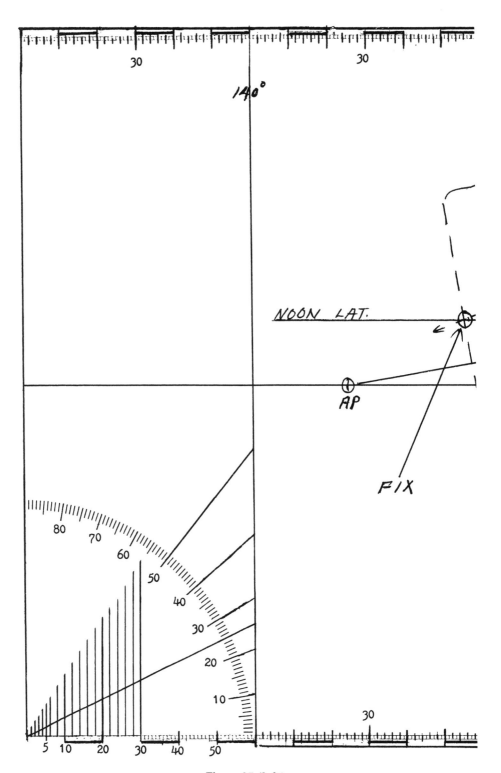

30

30

140°

NOON LAT.

AP

FIX

80
70
60
50
40
30
20
10

5 10 20 30 40 50

30

Figure 27 (left)

42

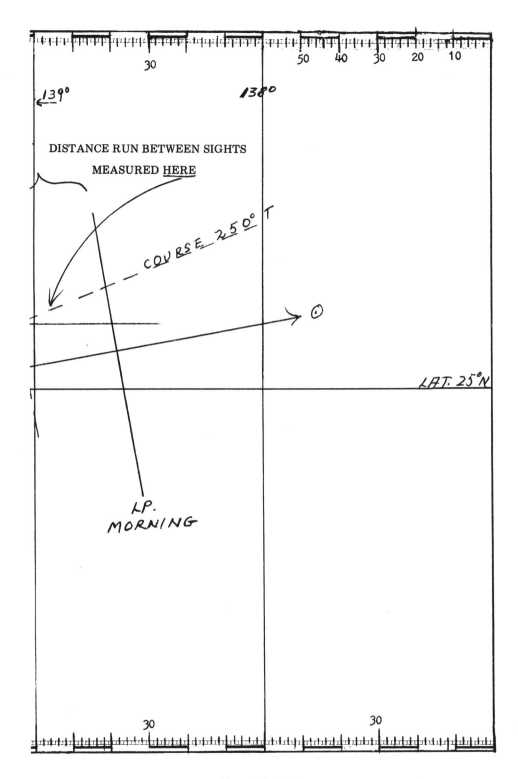

30

50 40 30 20 10

←139°   138°

DISTANCE RUN BETWEEN SIGHTS
MEASURED HERE

COURSE 250° T

O

LAT. 25°N

LP.
MORNING

30   30

Figure 27 (right)

43

WORK SHEET ---------- SOLAR SYSTEM

DATE *May 15 1972*   MILES RUN LAST POSITION _____
COURSE *045° T*   MILES MADE GOOD _____
LOG _____   TOTAL MILES RUN _____ MILES TO GO ___

1- DR Lat. *4° 30' S* DR Long. *148° 40' E* COMPUTED: Lat. _____ Long. _____

2- IC *-0.2'* HE *10'*	IC _____ HE _____	IC _____ HE _____
3- Body *⊙*	Body _____	Body _____
4- Hs *29° 15.3'*	Hs _____	Hs _____
5- IC & HE - *3.3*	IC & HE _____	IC & HE _____
6- App. Alt. *29° 12.0*	App. Alt. _____	App. Alt. _____
7- corr. *+ 14.3*	corr. _____	corr. _____
8- Ho *29° 26.3*	Ho _____	Ho _____

TIME OF OBSERVATION

9- *15* d *08* h *15* m *12* s	___ d ___ h ___ m ___ s	___ d ___ h ___ m ___ s
10- watch corr. *0*	watch corr. _____	watch corr. _____
11- GMT *14* d *22* h *15* m *12* s	GMT ___ d ___ h ___ m ___ s	GMT ___ d ___ h ___ m ___ s

DECLINATION --- FROM ALMANAC

12- mo.-day-hour *18° 49.3' N*	mo.-day-hour _____	mo.-day-hour _____
13- code d *0.6* corr. *⊕ 0.2'*	code d ___ corr. ± _____	code d ___ corr. ± _____
14- DEC. *18° 49.5*	DEC. _____	DEC. _____

GHA ------------FROM ALMANAC

15- mo.-day-hour *150° 55.6'*	mo.-day-hour _____	mo.-day-hour _____
16- min.-sec. *3 48.0*	min.-sec. _____	min.-sec. _____
17- code v ___ corr±	code v ___ corr± _____	code v ___ corr± _____
18- GHA *154° 43.6'*	GHA _____	GHA _____
19- Ass. Long. *148° 16.4*	Ass. Long. _____	Ass. Long. _____
20- LHA *303°*	LHA _____	LHA _____
21- Ass. Lat. *4° S*	Ass. Lat. _____	Ass. Lat. _____
22- Ass. Dec. *18° N*	Ass. Dec. _____	Ass. Dec. _____
23- Dec. remainder *49.5'*	Dec. remainder _____	Dec. remainder _____

FROM HO 249

24- Hc *29.41* d *17* Z *113*	Hc _____ d ___ Z ___	Hc _____ d ___ Z ___
25- corr *⊕ 14* , Zn *67°*	corr± _____ Zn ___	corr± _____ Zn ___
26- Hc *29° 27.0*	Hc _____	Hc _____
27- Ho *29° 26.3*	Ho _____	Ho _____
28- *.7* Ⓐ or T	A or T	A or T

Figure 28

45

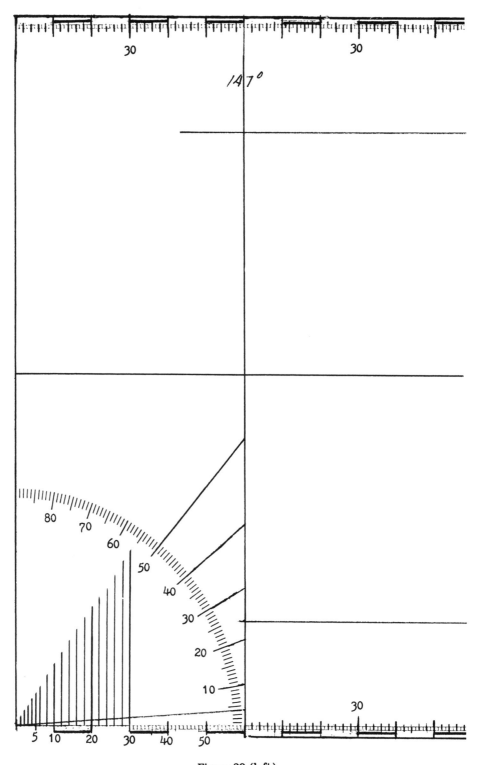

Figure 29 (left)

46

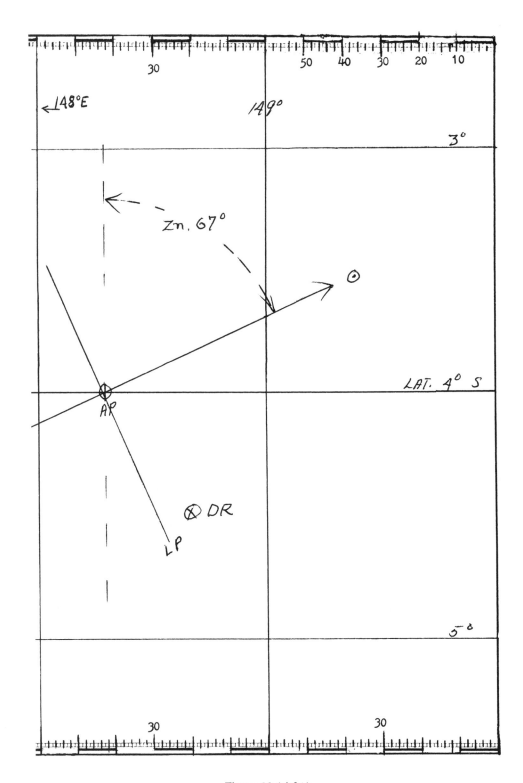

Figure 29 (right)

47

G.M.T.	SUN G.H.A.	SUN Dec.	MOON G.H.A.	v	MOON Dec.	d	H.P.
d h	° ′	° ′	° ′	′	° ′	′	′
19 00	179 05.4	N12 49.1	71 19.8	9.9	S 26 04.6	0.6	54.7
01	194 05.5	48.3	85 48.7	9.9	26 05.2	0.6	54.7
02	209 05.7	47.5	100 17.6	9.8	26 05.8	0.4	54.8
03	224 05.8	.. 46.7	114 46.4	9.8	26 06.2	0.3	54.8
04	239 06.0	45.8	129 15.2	9.8	26 06.5	0.1	54.8
05	254 06.1	45.0	143 44.0	9.7	26 06.6	0.0	54.8
06	269 06.2	N12 44.2	158 12.7	9.7	S 26 06.6	0.1	54.8
07	284 06.4	43.4	172 41.4	9.7	26 06.5	0.2	54.8
S 08	299 06.5	42.6	187 10.1	9.7	26 06.3	0.4	54.9
A 09	314 06.6	.. 41.8	201 38.8	9.7	26 05.9	0.5	54.9
T 10	329 06.8	40.9	216 07.5	9.6	26 05.4	0.7	54.9
U 11	344 07.0	40.1	230 36.1	9.6	26 04.7	0.7	54.9
R 12	359 07.1	N12 39.3	245 04.7	9.6	S 26 04.0	0.9	54.9
D 13	14 07.3	38.5	259 33.3	9.6	26 03.1	1.1	55.0
A 14	29 07.4	37.7	274 01.9	9.5	26 02.0	1.1	55.0
Y 15	44 07.6	.. 36.8	288 30.4	9.6	26 00.9	1.3	55.0
16	59 07.7	36.0	302 59.0	9.5	25 59.6	1.5	55.0
17	74 07.8	35.2	317 27.5	9.5	25 58.1	1.6	55.0
18	89 08.0	N12 34.4	331 56.1	9.5	S 25 56.5	1.7	55.1
19	104 08.1	33.6	346 24.6	9.5	25 54.8	1.8	55.1
20	119 08.3	32.7	0 53.1	9.4	25 53.0	2.0	55.1
21	134 08.4	.. 31.9	15 21.5	9.5	25 51.0	2.1	55.1
22	149 08.6	31.1	29 50.0	9.5	25 48.9	2.2	55.2
23	164 08.7	30.3	44 18.5	9.4	25 46.7	2.4	55.2
20 00	179 08.9	N12 29.4	58 46.9	9.5	S 25 44.3	2.5	55.2
01	194 09.0	28.6	73 15.4	9.4	25 41.8	2.6	55.2
02	209 09.2	27.8	87 43.8	9.5	25 39.2	2.8	55.2
03	224 09.3	.. 27.0	102 12.3	9.4	25 36.4	2.9	55.3
04	239 09.5	26.2	116 40.7	9.5	25 33.5	3.0	55.3
05	254 09.6	25.3	131 09.2	9.4	25 30.5	3.2	55.3
06	269 09.7	N12 24.5	145 37.6	9.4	S 25 27.3	3.3	55.3
07	284 09.9	23.7	160 06.0	9.4	25 24.0	3.4	55.4
08	299 10.1	22.9	174 34.4	9.5	25 20.6	3.6	55.4
S 09	314 10.2	.. 22.0	189 02.9	9.4	25 17.0	3.7	55.4
U 10	329 10.4	21.2	203 31.3	9.4	25 13.3	3.8	55.4
N 11	344 10.5	20.4	217 59.7	9.5	25 09.5	4.0	55.5
D 12	359 10.7	N12 19.5	232 28.2	9.4	S 25 05.5	4.1	55.5
A 13	14 10.8	18.7	246 56.6	9.5	25 01.4	4.2	55.5
Y 14	29 11.0	17.9	261 25.1	9.4	24 57.2	4.4	55.5
15	44 11.1	.. 17.1	275 53.5	9.5	24 52.8	4.5	55.6
16	59 11.3	16.2	290 22.0	9.5	24 48.3	4.6	55.6
17	74 11.4	15.4	304 50.5	9.4	24 43.7	4.8	55.6
18	89 11.6	N12 14.6	319 18.9	9.5	S 24 38.9	4.9	55.6
19	104 11.7	13.8	333 47.4	9.5	24 34.0	5.0	55.7
20	119 11.9	12.9	348 15.9	9.5	24 29.0	5.2	55.7
21	134 12.0	.. 12.1	2 44.4	9.6	24 23.8	5.3	55.7
22	149 12.2	11.3	17 13.0	9.5	24 18.5	5.4	55.7
23	164 12.3	10.4	31 41.5	9.5	24 13.1	5.6	55.8
21 00	179 12.5	N12 09.6	46 10.0	9.6	S 24 07.5	5.7	55.8
01	194 12.7	08.8	60 38.6	9.6	24 01.8	5.8	55.8
02	209 12.8	07.9	75 07.2	9.6	23 56.0	5.9	55.8
03	224 13.0	.. 07.1	89 35.8	9.6	23 50.1	6.1	55.9
04	239 13.1	06.3	104 04.4	9.6	23 44.0	6.2	55.9
05	254 13.3	05.4	118 33.0	9.7	23 37.8	6.3	55.9
06	269 13.4	N12 04.6	133 01.7	9.6	S 23 31.5	6.5	56.0
07	284 13.6	03.8	147 30.3	9.7	23 25.0	6.6	56.0
08	299 13.7	02.9	161 59.0	9.7	23 18.4	6.7	56.0
M 09	314 13.9	.. 02.1	176 27.7	9.7	23 11.7	6.9	56.0
O 10	329 14.0	01.3	190 56.4	9.8	23 04.8	6.9	56.1
N 11	344 14.2	12 00.4	205 25.2	9.8	22 57.9	7.1	56.1
D 12	359 14.4	N11 59.6	219 54.0	9.8	S 22 50.8	7.2	56.1
A 13	14 14.5	58.8	234 22.8	9.8	22 43.6	7.4	56.1
Y 14	29 14.7	57.9	248 51.6	9.8	22 36.2	7.5	56.2
15	44 14.8	.. 57.1	263 20.4	9.9	22 28.7	7.6	56.2
16	59 15.0	56.3	277 49.3	9.9	22 21.1	7.7	56.2
17	74 15.1	55.4	292 18.2	9.9	22 13.4	7.8	56.3
18	89 15.3	N11 54.6	306 47.1	9.9	S 22 05.6	8.0	56.3
19	104 15.4	53.8	321 16.0	10.0	21 57.6	8.1	56.3
20	119 15.6	52.9	335 45.0	10.0	21 49.5	8.2	56.3
21	134 15.8	.. 52.1	350 14.0	10.0	21 41.3	8.3	56.4
22	149 15.9	51.2	4 43.0	10.0	21 33.0	8.5	56.4
23	164 16.1	50.4	19 12.0	10.1	21 24.5	8.5	56.4
	S.D. 15.8	d 0.8	S.D. 15.0		15.1		15.3

Lat.	Twilight Naut.	Twilight Civil	Sun-rise	Moonrise 19	20	21	22
°	h m	h m	h m	h m	h m	h m	h m
N 72	////	////	02 56	■	■	■	21 54
N 70	////	01 35	03 21	■	■	■	20 41
68	////	02 17	03 40	■	■	21 06	20 03
66	////	02 46	03 55	■	■	19 56	19 36
64	01 23	03 06	04 07	■	19 26	19 20	19 15
62	02 02	03 23	04 17	18 20	18 44	18 54	18 58
60	02 27	03 37	04 26	17 43	18 15	18 33	18 44
N 58	02 47	03 48	04 34	17 17	17 53	18 16	18 32
56	03 03	03 58	04 40	16 56	17 35	18 02	18 21
54	03 16	04 07	04 47	16 39	17 19	17 50	18 12
52	03 28	04 15	04 52	16 24	17 06	17 39	18 04
50	03 37	04 22	04 57	16 11	16 55	17 29	17 56
45	03 58	04 36	05 07	15 45	16 30	17 08	17 40
N 40	04 13	04 48	05 16	15 24	16 11	16 51	17 27
35	04 25	04 57	05 24	15 07	15 55	16 37	17 15
30	04 36	05 05	05 30	14 52	15 40	16 25	17 05
20	04 52	05 19	05 41	14 26	15 16	16 04	16 48
N 10	05 04	05 29	05 51	14 04	14 56	15 45	16 33
0	05 14	05 39	06 00	13 44	14 36	15 28	16 19
S 10	05 23	05 47	06 09	13 23	14 17	15 11	16 05
20	05 30	05 56	06 18	13 01	13 56	14 52	15 50
30	05 36	06 04	06 29	12 36	13 31	14 31	15 32
35	05 39	06 09	06 35	12 21	13 17	14 18	15 22
40	05 42	06 14	06 41	12 04	13 01	14 04	15 10
45	05 45	06 19	06 49	11 43	12 41	13 46	14 57
S 50	05 48	06 25	06 59	11 16	12 16	13 25	14 40
52	05 49	06 28	07 03	11 03	12 04	13 14	14 31
54	05 50	06 31	07 08	10 49	11 50	13 03	14 23
56	05 51	06 34	07 13	10 32	11 34	12 50	14 12
58	05 52	06 38	07 19	10 11	11 15	12 34	14 01
S 60	05 53	06 42	07 26	09 45	10 51	12 15	13 47

Lat.	Sun-set	Twilight Civil	Twilight Naut.	Moonset 19	20	21	22
°	h m	h m	h m	h m	h m	h m	h m
N 72	21 06	////	////	■	■	■	23 29
N 70	20 42	22 24	////	■	■	■	■
68	20 24	21 44	////	■	■	22 28	25 17
66	20 10	21 18	////	■	22 18	23 37	25 43
64	19 58	20 57	22 36	■	22 18	24 12	00 12
62	19 48	20 41	22 01	21 35	23 00	24 38	00 38
60	19 39	20 28	21 36	22 12	23 29	24 58	00 58
N 58	19 31	20 16	21 17	22 38	23 50	25 14	01 14
56	19 25	20 07	21 02	22 59	24 08	00 08	01 28
54	19 19	19 58	20 48	23 16	24 23	00 23	01 40
52	19 14	19 51	20 37	23 30	24 36	00 36	01 50
50	19 09	19 44	20 28	23 43	24 48	00 48	02 00
45	18 58	19 30	20 08	24 09	00 09	01 11	02 19
N 40	18 50	19 18	19 53	24 30	00 30	01 30	02 35
35	18 43	19 09	19 40	24 47	00 47	01 46	02 49
30	18 36	19 01	19 30	00 09	01 02	02 00	03 00
20	18 25	18 48	19 14	00 34	01 27	02 23	03 20
N 10	18 16	18 37	19 02	00 56	01 49	02 43	03 38
0	18 07	18 28	18 52	01 17	02 09	03 01	03 53
S 10	17 58	18 19	18 44	01 37	02 29	03 20	04 09
20	17 49	18 11	18 37	01 59	02 51	03 39	04 25
30	17 38	18 03	18 31	02 25	03 15	04 02	04 44
35	17 32	17 58	18 28	02 40	03 30	04 15	04 56
40	17 26	17 53	18 25	02 57	03 47	04 30	05 08
45	17 18	17 48	18 22	03 18	04 07	04 49	05 23
S 50	17 09	17 42	18 20	03 45	04 32	05 11	05 41
52	17 04	17 39	18 19	03 57	04 45	05 22	05 50
54	17 00	17 36	18 18	04 12	04 59	05 34	05 59
56	16 54	17 33	18 17	04 29	05 15	05 47	06 10
58	16 49	17 30	18 16	04 50	05 34	06 03	06 22
S 60	16 42	17 26	18 15	05 16	05 58	06 22	06 37

Day	SUN Eqn. of Time 00h	12h	Mer. Pass.	MOON Mer. Pass. Upper	Lower	Age	Phase
	m s	m s	h m	h m	h m	d	
19	03 39	03 32	12 04	19 56	07 30	10	
20	03 25	03 18	12 03	20 49	08 22	11	○
21	03 10	03 03	12 03	21 40	09 15	12	

Figure 30

INCREMENTS AND CORRECTIONS

41^m

	SUN PLANETS	ARIES	MOON	v or Corrⁿ d	v or Corrⁿ d	v or Corrⁿ d
	° ′	° ′	° ′	′ ′	′ ′	′ ′
00	10 00·0	10 01·6	9 32·7	0·0 0·0	6·0 4·1	12·0 8·1
01	10 00·3	10 01·9	9 32·9	0·1 0·1	6·1 4·1	12·1 8·2
02	10 00·5	10 02·1	9 33·1	0·2 0·1	6·2 4·2	12·2 8·2
03	10 00·8	10 02·4	9 33·4	0·3 0·2	6·3 4·3	12·3 8·3
04	10 01·0	10 02·6	9 33·6	0·4 0·3	6·4 4·3	12·4 8·4
05	10 01·3	10 02·9	9 33·9	0·5 0·3	6·5 4·4	12·5 8·4
06	10 01·5	10 03·1	9 34·1	0·6 0·4	6·6 4·5	12·6 8·5
07	10 01·8	10 03·4	9 34·3	0·7 0·5	6·7 4·5	12·7 8·6
08	10 02·0	10 03·6	9 34·6	0·8 0·5	6·8 4·6	12·8 8·6
09	10 02·3	10 03·9	9 34·8	0·9 0·6	6·9 4·7	12·9 8·7
10	10 02·5	10 04·1	9 35·1	1·0 0·7	7·0 4·7	13·0 8·8
11	10 02·8	10 04·4	9 35·3	1·1 0·7	7·1 4·8	13·1 8·8
12	10 03·0	10 04·7	9 35·5	1·2 0·8	7·2 4·9	13·2 8·9
13	10 03·3	10 04·9	9 35·8	1·3 0·9	7·3 4·9	13·3 9·0
14	10 03·5	10 05·2	9 36·0	1·4 0·9	7·4 5·0	13·4 9·0
15	10 03·8	10 05·4	9 36·2	1·5 1·0	7·5 5·1	13·5 9·1
16	10 04·0	10 05·7	9 36·5	1·6 1·1	7·6 5·1	13·6 9·2
17	10 04·3	10 05·9	9 36·7	1·7 1·1	7·7 5·2	13·7 9·2
18	10 04·5	10 06·2	9 37·0	1·8 1·2	7·8 5·3	13·8 9·3
19	10 04·8	10 06·4	9 37·2	1·9 1·3	7·9 5·3	13·9 9·4
20	10 05·0	10 06·7	9 37·4	2·0 1·4	8·0 5·4	14·0 9·5
21	10 05·3	10 06·9	9 37·7	2·1 1·4	8·1 5·5	14·1 9·5
22	10 05·5	10 07·2	9 37·9	2·2 1·5	8·2 5·5	14·2 9·6
23	10 05·8	10 07·4	9 38·2	2·3 1·6	8·3 5·6	14·3 9·7
24	10 06·0	10 07·7	9 38·4	2·4 1·6	8·4 5·7	14·4 9·7
25	10 06·3	10 07·9	9 38·6	2·5 1·7	8·5 5·7	14·5 9·8
26	10 06·5	10 08·2	9 38·9	2·6 1·8	8·6 5·8	14·6 9·9
27	10 06·8	10 08·4	9 39·1	2·7 1·8	8·7 5·9	14·7 9·9
28	10 07·0	10 08·7	9 39·3	2·8 1·9	8·8 5·9	14·8 10·0
29	10 07·3	10 08·9	9 39·6	2·9 2·0	8·9 6·0	14·9 10·1
30	10 07·5	10 09·2	9 39·8	3·0 2·0	9·0 6·1	15·0 10·1
31	10 07·8	10 09·4	9 40·1	3·1 2·1	9·1 6·1	15·1 10·2
32	10 08·0	10 09·7	9 40·3	3·2 2·2	9·2 6·2	15·2 10·3
33	10 08·3	10 09·9	9 40·5	3·3 2·2	9·3 6·3	15·3 10·3
34	10 08·5	10 10·2	9 40·8	3·4 2·3	9·4 6·3	15·4 10·4
35	10 08·8	10 10·4	9 41·0	3·5 2·4	9·5 6·4	15·5 10·5
36	10 09·0	10 10·7	9 41·3	3·6 2·4	9·6 6·5	15·6 10·5
37	10 09·3	10 10·9	9 41·5	3·7 2·5	9·7 6·5	15·7 10·6
38	10 09·5	10 11·2	9 41·7	3·8 2·6	9·8 6·6	15·8 10·7
39	10 09·8	10 11·4	9 42·0	3·9 2·6	9·9 6·7	15·9 10·7
40	10 10·0	10 11·7	9 42·2	4·0 2·7	10·0 6·8	16·0 10·8
41	10 10·3	10 11·9	9 42·4	4·1 2·8	10·1 6·8	16·1 10·9
42	10 10·5	10 12·2	9 42·7	4·2 2·8	10·2 6·9	16·2 10·9
43	10 10·8	10 12·4	9 42·9	4·3 2·9	10·3 7·0	16·3 11·0
44	10 11·0	10 12·7	9 43·2	4·4 3·0	10·4 7·0	16·4 11·1
45	10 11·3	10 12·9	9 43·4	4·5 3·0	10·5 7·1	16·5 11·1
46	10 11·5	10 13·2	9 43·6	4·6 3·1	10·6 7·2	16·6 11·2
47	10 11·8	10 13·4	9 43·9	4·7 3·2	10·7 7·2	16·7 11·3
48	10 12·0	10 13·7	9 44·1	4·8 3·2	10·8 7·3	16·8 11·3
49	10 12·3	10 13·9	9 44·4	4·9 3·3	10·9 7·4	16·9 11·4
50	10 12·5	10 14·2	9 44·6	5·0 3·4	11·0 7·4	17·0 11·5
51	10 12·8	10 14·4	9 44·8	5·1 3·4	11·1 7·5	17·1 11·5
52	10 13·0	10 14·7	9 45·1	5·2 3·5	11·2 7·6	17·2 11·6
53	10 13·3	10 14·9	9 45·3	5·3 3·6	11·3 7·6	17·3 11·7
54	10 13·5	10 15·2	9 45·6	5·4 3·6	11·4 7·7	17·4 11·7
55	10 13·8	10 15·4	9 45·8	5·5 3·7	11·5 7·8	17·5 11·8
56	10 14·0	10 15·7	9 46·0	5·6 3·8	11·6 7·8	17·6 11·9
57	10 14·3	10 15·9	9 46·3	5·7 3·8	11·7 7·9	17·7 11·9
58	10 14·5	10 16·2	9 46·5	5·8 3·9	11·8 8·0	17·8 12·0
59	10 14·8	10 16·4	9 46·7	5·9 4·0	11·9 8·0	17·9 12·1
60	10 15·0	10 16·7	9 47·0	6·0 4·1	12·0 8·1	18·0 12·2

41^m	SUN PLANETS	ARIES	MOON	v or Corrⁿ d	v or Corrⁿ d	v or Corrⁿ d
s	° ′	° ′	° ′	′ ′	′ ′	′ ′
00	10 15·0	10 16·7	9 47·0	0·0 0·0	6·0 4·2	12·0 8·3
01	10 15·3	10 16·9	9 47·2	0·1 0·1	6·1 4·2	12·1 8·4
02	10 15·5	10 17·2	9 47·5	0·2 0·1	6·2 4·3	12·2 8·4
03	10 15·8	10 17·4	9 47·7	0·3 0·2	6·3 4·4	12·3 8·5
04	10 16·0	10 17·7	9 47·9	0·4 0·3	6·4 4·4	12·4 8·6
05	10 16·3	10 17·9	9 48·2	0·5 0·3	6·5 4·5	12·5 8·6
06	10 16·5	10 18·2	9 48·4	0·6 0·4	6·6 4·6	12·6 8·7
07	10 16·8	10 18·4	9 48·7	0·7 0·5	6·7 4·6	12·7 8·8
08	10 17·0	10 18·7	9 48·9	0·8 0·6	6·8 4·7	12·8 8·9
09	10 17·3	10 18·9	9 49·1	0·9 0·6	6·9 4·8	12·9 8·9
10	10 17·5	10 19·2	9 49·4	1·0 0·7	7·0 4·8	13·0 9·0
11	10 17·8	10 19·4	9 49·6	1·1 0·8	7·1 4·9	13·1 9·1
12	10 18·0	10 19·7	9 49·8	1·2 0·8	7·2 5·0	13·2 9·1
13	10 18·3	10 19·9	9 50·1	1·3 0·9	7·3 5·0	13·3 9·2
14	10 18·5	10 20·2	9 50·3	1·4 1·0	7·4 5·1	13·4 9·3
15	10 18·8	10 20·4	9 50·6	1·5 1·0	7·5 5·2	13·5 9·3
16	10 19·0	10 20·7	9 50·8	1·6 1·1	7·6 5·3	13·6 9·4
17	10 19·3	10 20·9	9 51·0	1·7 1·2	7·7 5·3	13·7 9·5
18	10 19·5	10 21·2	9 51·3	1·8 1·2	7·8 5·4	13·8 9·5
19	10 19·8	10 21·4	9 51·5	1·9 1·3	7·9 5·5	13·9 9·6
20	10 20·0	10 21·7	9 51·8	2·0 1·4	8·0 5·5	14·0 9·7
21	10 20·3	10 21·9	9 52·0	2·1 1·5	8·1 5·6	14·1 9·8
22	10 20·5	10 22·2	9 52·2	2·2 1·5	8·2 5·7	14·2 9·8
23	10 20·8	10 22·4	9 52·5	2·3 1·6	8·3 5·7	14·3 9·9
24	10 21·0	10 22·7	9 52·7	2·4 1·7	8·4 5·8	14·4 10·0
25	10 21·3	10 23·0	9 52·9	2·5 1·7	8·5 5·9	14·5 10·0
26	10 21·5	10 23·2	9 53·2	2·6 1·8	8·6 5·9	14·6 10·1
27	10 21·8	10 23·5	9 53·4	2·7 1·9	8·7 6·0	14·7 10·2
28	10 22·0	10 23·7	9 53·7	2·8 1·9	8·8 6·1	14·8 10·2
29	10 22·3	10 24·0	9 53·9	2·9 2·0	8·9 6·2	14·9 10·3
30	10 22·5	10 24·2	9 54·1	3·0 2·1	9·0 6·2	15·0 10·4
31	10 22·8	10 24·5	9 54·4	3·1 2·1	9·1 6·3	15·1 10·4
32	10 23·0	10 24·7	9 54·6	3·2 2·2	9·2 6·4	15·2 10·5
33	10 23·3	10 25·0	9 54·9	3·3 2·3	9·3 6·4	15·3 10·6
34	10 23·5	10 25·2	9 55·1	3·4 2·4	9·4 6·5	15·4 10·7
35	10 23·8	10 25·5	9 55·3	3·5 2·4	9·5 6·6	15·5 10·7
36	10 24·0	10 25·7	9 55·6	3·6 2·5	9·6 6·6	15·6 10·8
37	10 24·3	10 26·0	9 55·8	3·7 2·6	9·7 6·7	15·7 10·9
38	10 24·5	10 26·2	9 56·1	3·8 2·6	9·8 6·8	15·8 10·9
39	10 24·8	10 26·5	9 56·3	3·9 2·7	9·9 6·8	15·9 11·0
40	10 25·0	10 26·7	9 56·5	4·0 2·8	10·0 6·9	16·0 11·1
41	10 25·3	10 27·0	9 56·8	4·1 2·8	10·1 7·0	16·1 11·1
42	10 25·5	10 27·2	9 57·0	4·2 2·9	10·2 7·1	16·2 11·2
43	10 25·8	10 27·5	9 57·2	4·3 3·0	10·3 7·1	16·3 11·3
44	10 26·0	10 27·7	9 57·5	4·4 3·0	10·4 7·2	16·4 11·3
45	10 26·3	10 28·0	9 57·7	4·5 3·1	10·5 7·3	16·5 11·4
46	10 26·5	10 28·2	9 58·0	4·6 3·2	10·6 7·3	16·6 11·5
47	10 26·8	10 28·5	9 58·2	4·7 3·3	10·7 7·4	16·7 11·6
48	10 27·0	10 28·7	9 58·4	4·8 3·3	10·8 7·5	16·8 11·6
49	10 27·3	10 29·0	9 58·7	4·9 3·4	10·9 7·5	16·9 11·7
50	10 27·5	10 29·2	9 58·9	5·0 3·5	11·0 7·6	17·0 11·8
51	10 27·8	10 29·5	9 59·2	5·1 3·5	11·1 7·7	17·1 11·8
52	10 28·0	10 29·7	9 59·4	5·2 3·6	11·2 7·7	17·2 11·9
53	10 28·3	10 30·0	9 59·6	5·3 3·7	11·3 7·8	17·3 12·0
54	10 28·5	10 30·2	9 59·9	5·4 3·7	11·4 7·9	17·4 12·0
55	10 28·8	10 30·5	10 00·1	5·5 3·8	11·5 8·0	17·5 12·1
56	10 29·0	10 30·7	10 00·3	5·6 3·9	11·6 8·0	17·6 12·2
57	10 29·3	10 31·0	10 00·6	5·7 3·9	11·7 8·1	17·7 12·2
58	10 29·5	10 31·2	10 00·8	5·8 4·0	11·8 8·1	17·8 12·3
59	10 29·8	10 31·5	10 01·1	5·9 4·1	11·9 8·2	17·9 12·4
60	10 30·0	10 31·7	10 01·3	6·0 4·2	12·0 8·3	18·0 12·5

Figure 31

VIII. OTHER MEMBERS OF THE SOLAR SYSTEM

If you have your Sun shots down pat, and you should by now, planets will not be too hard to learn. The first problem is how to identify them. Planets are not always available, for a good part of the time they are in our sky during daylight, too close to the Sun, and cannot be seen. (Except that Venus can sometimes be found during daylight.) Somewhere in the first few pages of the *Almanac* you will find a section headed "PLANET NOTES." In my 1972 copy this is on pages 8 and 9. These pages include a chart indicating the position of the navigational planets for each hour of the day throughout the year. The chart is a quick reference indicating which of the planets are available to you and whether they will be useful at morning or evening twilight. They change during the year, sometimes quite rapidly. Read these notes carefully and study the chart until you understand it well. The instructions for use of the chart are complete on these pages.

It should be pointed out at this time that morning or evening twilight is the time for taking sights of planets or stars, although, as noted previously, Venus can sometimes be found during daylight. The proper time for the sight is after it has become dark enough to see the body, but before it has become too dark to see the horizon. There is sunrise-sunset, moonrise-moonset data on the right side of each right hand daily page in the *Almanac*. Explanatory data in the back of the *Almanac* tells you how to use it to predetermine twilight for your position.

There are three major differences between taking and computing a planet sight and a sun sight. They are:

One—In taking a sight of a planet (or a star) the body does not sit on the horizon as with the Sun, but is centered on the horizon.

Two—There are frequently "Additional Corrections" for Mars and Venus throughout the year. These corrections are in a separate column on the inside front cover of your *Almanac* just to the right of the column of regular corrections for stars and planets. They apply to the span of App. Alt. shown with each additional correction. During the dates when these corrections apply, the regular correction should be made first, and then the additional correction (Fig. 32A).

Three—With the planets, the "v" factor will apply as a correction to GHA. The code for "v" will be at the bottom of the column for the planets on the daily page. You must remember that this factor is always a plus (+) to GHA unless the "v" factor has a minus (-) sign before it at the bottom of the daily page. (This will happen only with Venus.) Now, let's go through a Venus sight step by step (Fig. 32B).

In this example, we are sailing down the eastern coast of the United States from New York to Miami. It is the twilight before dawn and Venus is bright in the eastern sky.

Now, to the work sheet:

Date: Aug. 28, 1972.
Line 1—My DR position is Lat. 39° 20'N., Long. 74° 00'W.

WORK SHEET ---------- SOLAR SYSTEM

DATE _Aug. 28, 1972_ MILES RUN LAST POSITION _____
COURSE _/_____ MILES MADE GOOD _____
LOG _____   TOTAL MILES RUN _____ MILES TO GO __

1- DR Lat. _39°20'N_ DR Long. _74°00'W_ COMPUTED: Lat. _____ Long. _____

2- IC _0_ HE _15'_	IC _____ HE _____	IC _____ HE _____
3- Body _☉_	Body _____	Body _____
4- Hs _28° 35.5'_	Hs _____	Hs _____
5- IC & HE _− 3.8_	IC & HE _____	IC & HE _____
6- App. Alt. _28° 31.7_	App. Alt. _____	App. Alt. _____
7- corr. _− 1.6_	corr. _____	corr. _____
8- Ho _28° 30.1'_	Ho _____	Ho _____

TIME OF OBSERVATION

9- _28_ d _05_ h _17_ m _10_ s	___ d ___ h ___ m ___ s	___ d ___ h ___ m ___ s
10- watch corr. _+ 45_	watch corr. _____	watch corr. _____
11- GMT _28_ d _09_ h _17_ m _14_ s	GMT ___ d ___ h ___ m ___ s	GMT ___ d ___ h ___ m ___ s

DECLINATION --- FROM ALMANAC

12- mo.-day-hour _19°13.3 N_	mo.-day-hour _____	mo.-day-hour _____
13- code d _0_ / corr ⊕ _0_	code d ___ corr.± _____	code d ___ corr.± _____
14- DEC. _19°13.3_	DEC. _____	DEC. _____

GHA ------------FROM ALMANAC

15- mo.-day-hour _1° 10.6'_	mo.-day-hour _____	mo.-day-hour _____
16- min.-sec. _4 18.5_	min.-sec. _____	min.-sec. _____
17- code v _0_ / corr ⊕ _0_	code v ___ corr± _____	code v ___ corr± _____
18- GHA _5°29.1_	GHA _____	GHA _____

19- Ass. Long. _74°29.1'_	Ass. Long. _____	Ass. Long. _____
20- LHA _291°_	LHA _____	LHA _____
21- Ass. Lat. _39° N_	Ass. Lat. _____	Ass. Lat. _____
22- Ass. Dec. _19° N_	Ass. Dec. _____	Ass. Dec. _____
23- Dec. remainder _13.3'_	Dec. remainder _____	Dec. remainder _____

FROM HO 249

24- Hc _27°55'_ d _34_ Z _88_	Hc _____ d ___ Z ___	Hc _____ d ___ Z ___
25- corr⊕ _70_ Zn _88_	corr± _____ Zn _____	corr± _____ Zn _____
26- Hc _28°02.0_	Hc _____	Hc _____
27- Ho _28°30.1_	Ho _____	Ho _____
28- _28.1_ A or (T)	_____ A or T	_____ A or T

Figure 32A

51

OCT.—MAR.	SUN	APR.—SEPT.		STARS AND PLANETS				DIP				
App. Alt.	Lower Limb Upper Limb	App. Alt.	Lower Limb Upper Limb	App. Alt.	Corrn	App. Alt.	Additional Corrn	Ht. of Eye	Corrn	Ht. of Eye	Ht. of Eye	Corrn
				9 56	−5.3	**1972**						
				10 08	−5.2	**VENUS**						
				10 20	−5.1	Jan.1–Feb.29						
				10 33	−5.0	0°						
				10 46	−4.9	42	+0.1					
				11 00	−4.8	Mar.1–Apr.15						
				11 14	−4.7	0°						
				11 29	−4.6	47	+0.2					
				11 45	−4.5	Apr.16–May12						
				12 01	−4.4	0°						
				12 18	−4.3	46	+0.3					
				12 35	−4.2	May13–May27						
				12 54	−4.1	0°						
				13 13	−4.0	11	+0.4					
				13 33	−3.9	41	+0.5					
				13 54	−3.8	May28–June5						
				14 16	−3.7	0°						
				14 40	−3.6	6	+0.5					
				15 04	−3.5	20	+0.6					
				15 30	−3.4	31	+0.7					
				15 57	−3.3	June6–June 29						
				16 26	−3.2	0°						
				16 56	−3.1	4	+0.6					
				17 28	−3.0	12	+0.7					
				18 02	−2.9	22	+0.8					
				18 38	−2.8	June 30–July 8						
				19 17	−2.7	0°						
				19 58	−2.6	6	+0.5					
				20 42	−2.5	20	+0.6					
				21 28	−2.4	31	+0.7					
				22 19	−2.3	July 9–July 24						
				23 13	−2.2	0°						
				24 11	−2.1	11	0.4					
				25 14	−2.0	41	0.5					
				26 22	−1.9	July25–Aug.19						
				27 36	−1.8	0°						
				28 56	−1.7	46	+0.3					
				30 24	−1.6	Aug.20–Oct.5						
				32 00	−1.5	0°						
				33 45	−1.4	47	0.2					
				35 40	−1.3	Oct.6–Dec. 31						
				37 48	−1.2	0°						
				40 08	−1.1	42	0.1					
				42 44	−1.0							
				45 36	−0.9							
				48 47	−0.8							
				52 18	−0.7	**MARS**						
				56 11	−0.6	Jan. 1–Dec. 31						
				60 28	−0.5	0°						
				65 08	−0.4	60	+0.1					
				70 11	−0.3							
				75 34	−0.2							
				81 13	−0.1							
				87 03	0.0							
				90 00								

Additional Correction

App. Alt. = Apparent altitude = Sextant altitude corrected for index error and dip.

For daylight observations of Venus, see page 260.

Figure 32B

Line 2—No Index error, and an HE of 15 feet.

Line 3—The body is Venus. I have used her symbol.

Line 4—An Hs of 28° 35.5′ is obtained by splitting the horizon with Venus.

Line 5—Dip is recorded.

Line 6—I subtract dip and have my App. Alt.

Line 7—Now, one of the new problems. Looking down the corr. column for stars and planets for App. Alt. of 28° 31.7′ I find a correction of -1.8′. Looking to the right of that column I find, between Aug. 20 and Oct. 5, for App. Alt. readings between 0° and 47° there is an additional corr. of +0.2′. I put these together for a final corr. of -1.6′. This gives me on:

Line 8—An Ho of 28° 30.1′.

Line 9—The time of my sight was 5:17:10 a.m. Eastern Standard Time, and my watch was 4 sec. slow.

Line 10—Here is the watch error.

Line 11—The time is corrected and converted to GMT.

Line 12—In the *Almanac* to the Aug. 28 page and to the 9th hour GMT I find the Dec. for that hour.

Line 13—I look at the tenth hour and see that Dec. is decreasing so I circle the minus sign and check the bottom of the page for the "d" factor. I record it on this line.

Line 14—I didn't compute this until I had turned to the minute page and determined the value of "d" as zero. Then, my final Dec.

Line 15—Now, from the daily page I have my GHA for the 9th hour of GMT.

Line 16—Here is the change in GHA for the 17min. 14sec.

Line 17—Now we have the "v" code. This is picked up from the bottom of the page under the Venus column right next to the "d" code.

Line 18—My final GHA.

Line 19—My assumed Long. with the same minutes as in the GHA.

Line 20—My computed LHA. (Look up the formula.)

Line 21—I assume Lat. 39° as it is the nearest full degree.

Line 22—My assumed Dec. (an even degree).

Line 23—The Dec. remainder.

Line 24—Now, use the *H.O. 249 Vol. II* in the same way I did for the Sun. First, find the Latitude section, then the Dec. column in the *SAME* section, and finally the LHA line. At the coordinates I find Hc, d, and Z.

Line 25—This is the correction for "d" and the Dec. remainder I found in table No. 5. It is a +, because, reading at the next higher Dec. column from where I found the information on line 24, I found the Hc higher.

Line 26—My final Hc.

Line 27—Ho is brought down and I find it higher than Hc so I circle the "T" for Toward.

Line 28—And now I have the miles toward Venus from my assumed position. Back on line 25, to the far right, I have checked the formula in the top left corner of the page in *H.O. 249* and found that Z was equal to Zn. I recorded it here to use in my plot which is included (Fig. 33).

(Text continues on page 57.)

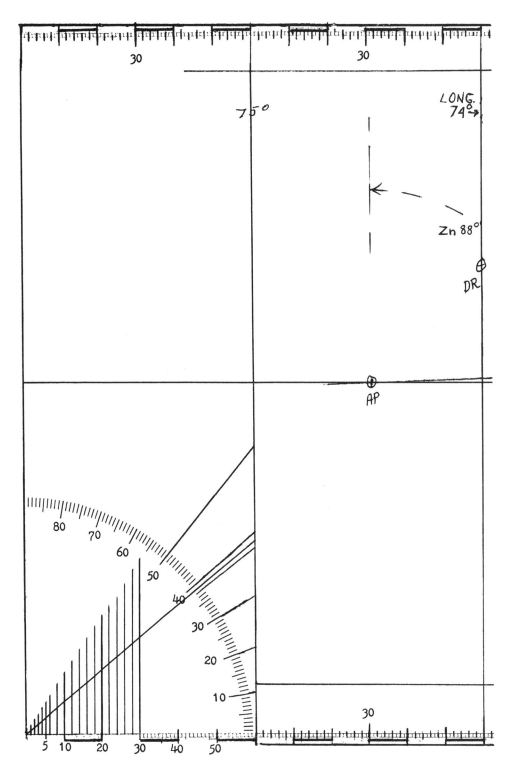

Figure 33 (left)

54

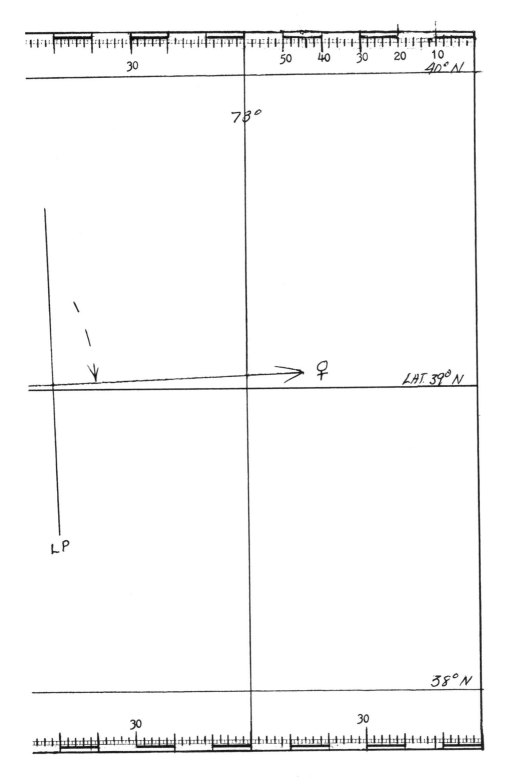

Figure 33 (right)

G.M.T.	ARIES G.H.A.	VENUS −4.0 G.H.A.	VENUS Dec.	MARS +2.0 G.H.A.	MARS Dec.	JUPITER −2.0 G.H.A.	JUPITER Dec.	SATURN +0.3 G.H.A.	SATURN Dec.	STARS Name	S.H.A.	Dec.
19 00	327 26·4	226 13·4	N19 24·3	172 33·1	N11 36·7	59 01·2	S23 22·7	249 25·7	N21 25·3	Acamar	315 41·3	S 40 24·4
01	342 28·9	241 13·5	24·4	187 34·0	36·1	74 03·7	22·8	264 28·0	25·3	Achernar	335 48·9	S 57 22·1
02	357 31·4	256 13·6	24·4	202 35·0	35·5	89 06·2	22·8	279 30·3	25·4	Acrux	173 44·4	S 62 57·1
03	12 33·8	271 13·7 ··	24·4	217 35·9 ··	34·9	104 08·8 ··	22·8	294 32·5 ··	25·4	Adhara	255 36·8	S 28 55·8
04	27 36·3	286 13·8	24·4	232 36·9	34·3	119 11·3	22·8	309 34·8	25·4	Aldebaran	291 24·6	N 16 27·5
05	42 38·8	301 13·9	24·5	247 37·9	33·8	134 13·8	22·8	324 37·1	25·4			
06	57 41·2	316 13·9	N19 24·5	262 38·8	N11 33·2	149 16·3	S23 22·8	339 39·3	N21 25·4	Alioth	166 47·6	N 56 06·6
07	72 43·7	331 14·0	24·5	277 39·8	32·6	164 18·8	22·8	354 41·6	25·4	Alkaid	153 23·0	N 49 27·1
S 08	87 46·2	346 14·1	24·5	292 40·7	32·0	179 21·3	22·8	9 43·9	25·4	Al Na'ir	28 21·4	S 47 05·5
A 09	102 48·6	1 14·2 ··	24·5	307 41·7 ··	31·5	194 23·9 ··	22·8	24 46·1 ··	25·4	Alnilam	276 17·6	S 1 12·9
T 10	117 51·1	16 14·3	24·6	322 42·6	30·9	209 26·4	22·8	39 48·4	25·5	Alphard	218 26·5	S 8 32·3
U 11	132 53·5	31 14·4	24·6	337 43·6	30·3	224 28·9	22·8	54 50·7	25·5			
R 12	147 56·0	46 14·5	N19 24·6	352 44·5	N11 29·7	239 31·4	S23 22·8	69 52·9	N21 25·5	Alphecca	126 36·9	N 26 48·5
D 13	162 58·5	61 14·6	24·6	7 45·5	29·1	254 33·9	22·8	84 55·2	25·5	Alpheratz	358 15·0	N 28 56·5
A 14	178 00·9	76 14·6	24·6	22 46·5	28·5	269 36·4	22·8	99 57·5	25·5	Altair	62 37·8	N 8 47·8
Y 15	193 03·4	91 14·7 ··	24·6	37 47·4 ··	28·0	284 38·9 ··	22·8	114 59·7 ··	25·5	Ankaa	353 45·3	S 42 26·9
16	208 05·9	106 14·8	24·6	52 48·4	27·4	299 41·5	22·8	130 02·0	25·5	Antares	113 03·8	S 26 22·7
17	223 08·3	121 14·9	24·7	67 49·3	26·8	314 44·0	22·8	145 04·2	25·5			
18	238 10·8	136 15·0	N19 24·7	82 50·3	N11 26·2	329 46·5	S23 22·8	160 06·5	N21 25·5	Arcturus	146 23·7	N 19 19·5
19	253 13·3	151 15·0	24·7	97 51·2	25·6	344 49·0	22·8	175 08·8	25·6	Atria	108 33·0	S 68 59·1
20	268 15·7	166 15·1	24·7	112 52·2	25·1	359 51·5	22·9	190 11·0	25·6	Avior	234 31·2	S 59 25·1
21	283 18·2	181 15·2 ··	24·7	127 53·1 ··	24·5	14 54·0 ··	22·9	205 13·3 ··	25·6	Bellatrix	279 05·0	N 6 19·7
22	298 20·7	196 15·3	24·7	142 54·1	23·9	29 56·5	22·9	220 15·6	25·6	Betelgeuse	271 34·6	N 7 24·3
23	313 23·1	211 15·3	24·7	157 55·1	23·3	44 59·0	22·9	235 17·9	25·6			
20 00	328 25·6	226 15·4	N19 24·7	172 56·0	N11 22·7	60 01·5	S23 22·9	250 20·1	N21 25·6	Canopus	264 10·1	S 52 40·5
01	343 28·0	241 15·5	24·8	187 57·0	22·2	75 04·0	22·9	265 22·4	25·6	Capella	281 19·9	N 45 58·3
02	358 30·5	256 15·5	24·8	202 57·9	21·6	90 06·6	22·9	280 24·7	25·6	Deneb	49 52·0	N 45 11·1
03	13 33·0	271 15·6 ··	24·8	217 58·9 ··	21·0	105 09·1 ··	22·9	295 26·9 ··	25·7	Denebola	183 05·0	N 14 43·5
04	28 35·4	286 15·7	24·8	232 59·8	20·4	120 11·6	22·9	310 29·2	25·7	Diphda	349 26·3	S 18 07·9
05	43 37·9	301 15·7	24·8	248 00·8	19·8	135 14·1	22·9	325 31·5	25·7			
06	58 40·4	316 15·8	N19 24·8	263 01·8	N11 19·2	150 16·6	S23 22·9	340 33·7	N21 25·7	Dubhe	194 29·4	N 61 54·0
07	73 42·8	331 15·9	24·8	278 02·7	18·7	165 19·1	22·9	355 36·0	25·7	Elnath	278 51·5	N 28 35·2
08	88 45·3	346 15·9	24·8	293 03·7	18·1	180 21·6	22·9	10 38·3	25·7	Eltanin	91 00·1	N 51 29·7
S 09	103 47·8	1 16·0 ··	24·8	308 04·6 ··	17·5	195 24·1 ··	22·9	25 40·5 ··	25·7	Enif	34 16·8	N 9 45·1
U 10	118 50·2	16 16·1	24·8	323 05·6	16·9	210 26·6	22·9	40 42·8	25·7	Fomalhaut	15 57·2	S 29 45·8
N 11	133 52·7	31 16·1	24·8	338 06·5	16·3	225 29·1	22·9	55 45·1	25·7			
D 12	148 55·2	46 16·2	N19 24·8	353 07·5	N11 15·7	240 31·6	S23 22·9	70 47·3	N21 25·8	Gacrux	172 35·7	S 56 57·8
A 13	163 57·6	61 16·2	24·8	8 08·5	15·2	255 34·1	22·9	85 49·6	25·8	Gienah	176 24·1	S 17 23·5
Y 14	179 00·1	76 16·3	24·8	23 09·4	14·6	270 36·6	22·9	100 51·9	25·8	Hadar	149 31·9	S 60 14·8
15	194 02·5	91 16·4 ··	24·8	38 10·4 ··	14·0	285 39·1 ··	23·0	115 54·1 ··	25·8	Hamal	328 35·2	N 23 20·1
16	209 05·0	106 16·4	24·8	53 11·3	13·4	300 41·6	23·0	130 56·4	25·8	Kaus Aust.	84 24·1	S 34 24·1
17	224 07·5	121 16·5	24·8	68 12·3	12·8	315 44·2	23·0	145 58·7	25·8			
18	239 09·9	136 16·5	N19 24·8	83 13·2	N11 12·2	330 46·7	S23 23·0	161 01·0	N21 25·8	Kochab	137 18·6	N 74 16·2
19	254 12·4	151 16·6	24·8	98 14·2	11·7	345 49·2	23·0	176 03·2	25·8	Markab	14 08·5	N 15 03·6
20	269 14·9	166 16·6	24·8	113 15·2	11·1	0 51·7	23·0	191 05·5	25·9	Menkar	314 47·0	N 3 59·2
21	284 17·3	181 16·7 ··	24·8	128 16·1 ··	10·5	15 54·2 ··	23·0	206 07·8 ··	25·9	Menkent	148 43·9	S 36 14·4
22	299 19·8	196 16·7	24·8	143 17·1	09·9	30 56·7	23·0	221 10·0	25·9	Miaplacidus	221 47·4	S 69 36·2
23	314 22·3	211 16·8	24·8	158 18·0	09·3	45 59·2	23·0	236 12·3	25·9			
21 00	329 24·7	226 16·8	N19 24·8	173 19·0	N11 08·7	61 01·7	S23 23·0	251 14·6	N21 25·9	Mirfak	309 24·3	N 49 45·9
01	344 27·2	241 16·9	24·8	188 20·0	08·1	76 04·2	23·0	266 16·9	25·9	Nunki	76 35·9	S 26 20·0
02	359 29·7	256 16·9	24·8	203 20·9	07·6	91 06·7	23·0	281 19·1	25·9	Peacock	54 06·6	S 56 49·5
03	14 32·1	271 16·9 ··	24·8	218 21·9 ··	07·0	106 09·2 ··	23·0	296 21·4 ··	25·9	Pollux	244 05·4	N 28 05·7
04	29 34·6	286 17·0	24·8	233 22·8	06·4	121 11·7	23·0	311 23·7	25·9	Procyon	245 32·0	N 5 17·9
05	44 37·0	301 17·0	24·8	248 23·8	05·8	136 14·2	23·0	326 25·9	26·0			
06	59 39·5	316 17·1	N19 24·8	263 24·8	N11 05·2	151 16·7	S23 23·0	341 28·2	N21 26·0	Rasalhague	96 34·7	N 12 34·8
07	74 42·0	331 17·1	24·7	278 25·7	04·6	166 19·2	23·0	356 30·5	26·0	Regulus	208 16·3	N 12 06·1
08	89 44·4	346 17·2	24·7	293 26·7	04·1	181 21·7	23·0	11 32·8	26·0	Rigel	281 41·6	S 8 13·7
M 09	104 46·9	1 17·2 ··	24·7	308 27·6 ··	03·5	196 24·2 ··	23·0	26 35·0 ··	26·0	Rigil Kent.	140 33·9	S 60 43·7
O 10	119 49·4	16 17·2	24·7	323 28·6	02·9	211 26·7	23·1	41 37·3	26·0	Sabik	102 47·5	S 15 41·6
N 11	134 51·8	31 17·3	24·7	338 29·6	02·3	226 29·2	23·1	56 39·6	26·0			
D 12	149 54·3	46 17·3	N19 24·7	353 30·5	N11 01·7	241 31·7	S23 23·1	71 41·9	N21 26·0	Schedar	350 15·3	N 56 23·3
A 13	164 56·8	61 17·3	24·7	8 31·5	01·1	256 34·2	23·1	86 44·1	26·0	Shaula	97 03·3	S 37 05·3
Y 14	179 59·2	76 17·4	24·7	23 32·4	11 00·5	271 36·6	23·1	101 46·4	26·1	Sirius	259 00·9	S 16 40·5
15	195 01·7	91 17·4 ··	24·6	38 33·4	10 59·9	286 39·1 ··	23·1	116 48·7 ··	26·1	Spica	159 03·7	S 11 01·2
16	210 04·1	106 17·4	24·6	53 34·4	59·4	301 41·6	23·1	131 50·9	26·1	Suhail	223 15·5	S 43 19·2
17	225 06·6	121 17·5	24·6	68 35·3	58·8	316 44·1	23·1	146 53·2	26·1			
18	240 09·1	136 17·5	N19 24·6	83 36·3	N10 58·2	331 46·6	S23 23·1	161 55·5	N21 26·1	Vega	80 59·4	N 38 45·6
19	255 11·5	151 17·5	24·6	98 37·2	57·6	346 49·1	23·1	176 57·8	26·1	Zuben'ubi	137 39·4	S 15 55·8
20	270 14·0	166 17·5	24·6	113 38·2	57·0	1 51·6	23·1	192 00·0	26·1			
21	285 16·5	181 17·6 ··	24·5	128 39·2 ··	56·4	16 54·1 ··	23·1	207 02·3 ··	26·1		S.H.A.	Mer. Pass.
22	300 18·9	196 17·6	24·5	143 40·1	55·8	31 56·6	23·1	222 04·6	26·1	Venus	257 49·8	8 55
23	315 21·4	211 17·6	24·5	158 41·1	55·2	46 59·1	23·1	237 06·9	26·2	Mars	204 30·4	12 27
										Jupiter	91 36·0	19 57
Mer. Pass. 2 05·9		v 0·1 d 0·0		v 1·0 d 0·6		v 2·5 d 0·0		v 2·3 d 0·0		Saturn	281 54·5	7 18

Figure 34

You now have another work sheet, Fig. 32B, with two blank spaces. One space is for the planet you find and shoot, the other is to solve the following problem:

The date is Aug. 19, 1972 and you left San Francisco early in the morning and headed west. You suspect that current is setting you a bit south of west. You've had a good reach all day and it is now evening twilight. You spot Jupiter in the south-southeast bright and shiny in the evening sky so you go for your sextant. Here is the information you collect from one source or another:

IC = 0.2 (-).
HE = 10 feet.
Hs = 25° 28.8′.
Time = 19:40:25 PC DLS (A word of caution, watch for the date change
          when converting to GMT.)
No watch error.
DR = Lat. 37° 00′N., Long. 124° 30′W.

(The answer is 8.5 Mi. Away.)

IX. MOON

A look at the width of the Moon column in the daily pages of the *Almanac* will tip you off right away that there is a vast number of corrections in this romantic hunk of heaven. Don't let that frighten you away though, because the Moon can be helpful. As mentioned earlier, she is often there when the Sun is up and thus gives us two bodies for a quick fix during the daytime. She is also easy to find and sight so let's go to work.

Figure 35A is another work sheet with a sight worked to a line of position for the Moon.

This time I am cruising among the Hawaiian Islands and am between Molokai and Oahu when I notice that both the Sun and Moon are out and shining. It is a morning Sun and an afternoon Moon. I take a sight of the Moon at 10:42:05 a.m. by my watch which I find to be 8 seconds fast.

Line 1—Work sheet gives my DR.
Line 2—IC and HE are recorded.
Line 3—My Hs is recorded.
Line 4—My Dip is determined, recorded and,
Line 5—Subtracted for an App. Alt. on,
Line 6—The App. Alt. is 37° 19.9′.
Line 7—Up to now everything has been as usual but look at the size of that corr. on this line. You will have noticed that there is no "Moon" column on the inside front cover of the *Almanac*. Corrections for the moon are on the last page and the inside back cover. Turn there and let us have a look. Across the top of the left-hand page are column headings for App. Alt. from 0° to 34° in brackets of 5 degrees. The right hand side is the same for App. Alt. from 35° to 89°. Our App. Alt. is 37° 19.9′ so let's look at the first five-degree column on the right hand page where our 37° falls. (Fig. 35B). Looking down that column you will find each of the five degrees, and then referring to the boldface numbers at the extreme left of the page you will find minutes by tens. We pick the 37 degrees and the minute line closest to ours. This would be 20′. Opposite that we find 55.2′. This is the first part of our correction on line 7 of the work sheet.

Now, for the rest of it turn to the daily page for the date of our sight and then down to the hour (GMT). You will note five columns of numbers in the moon column. They are GHA, "v," Dec., "d" and H.P. The H.P. is the new one, and the one we want now. You don't have to understand what H.P. is in order to navigate on the sea, but if you are curious here is a little information on the subject. H.P. stands for Horizontal Parallax and it has to do with the difference in the Apparent Altitude of a celestial body as viewed from the surface of the earth, and the center of the earth. The moon is so close to us that this difference makes a difference and has to be accounted for when correcting moon shots.

WORK SHEET ---------- SOLAR SYSTEM

Corr. 55.2

57.7 — H.P. *5.0*
60.2

DATE _April 8, 1972_   MILES RUN LAST POSITION _____
COURSE _____   MILES MADE GOOD _____
LOG _____   TOTAL MILES RUN _____ MILES TO GO _____

1- DR Lat. _21°10' N_ DR Long. _157°30' W_ COMPUTED: Lat. _____ Long. _____

2- IC _0_ HE _9'_	IC _____ HE _____	IC _____ HE _____
3- Body _☾_	Body _____	Body _____
4- Hs _37°22.8'_	Hs _____	Hs _____
5- IC & HE — _2.9_	IC & HE _____	IC & HE _____
6- App. Alt. _37°19.9'_	App. Alt. _____	App. Alt. _____
7- corr. + _60.2_	corr. _____	corr. _____
8- Ho _38° 20.1'_	Ho _____	Ho _____

TIME OF OBSERVATION

9- _8_ d _10_ h _42_ m _5_ s	____ d ___ h ___ m ___ s	____ d ___ h ___ m ___ s
10- watch corr. — _85_	watch corr. _____	watch corr. _____
11- GMT _8_ d _20_ h _41_ m _57_ s	GMT ___ d ___ h ___ m ___ s	GMT ___ d ___ h ___ m ___ s

DECLINATION --- FROM ALMANAC

12- mo.-day-hour _16°38.2' S_	mo.-day-hour _____	mo.-day-hour _____
13- code d _11.9_ corr⊖ _8.2_	code d ___ corr.± ___	code d ___ corr.± ___
14- DEC. _16° 30.0'_	DEC. _____	DEC. _____

GHA -----------FROM ALMANAC

15- mo.-day-hour _183°45.6'_	mo.-day-hour _____	mo.-day-hour _____
16- min.-sec. _10 00 6_	min.-sec. _____	min.-sec. _____
17- code v _10.8_ corr⊕ _7.5_	code v ___ corr± ___	code v ___ corr± ___
18- GHA _193° 53.7'_	GHA _____	GHA _____
19- Ass. Long. _157° 53.7'_	Ass. Long. _____	Ass. Long. _____
20- LHA _36°_	LHA _____	LHA _____
21- Ass. Lat. _21° N_	Ass. Lat. _____	Ass. Lat. _____
22- Ass. Dec. _16° S_	Ass. Dec. _____	Ass. Dec. _____
23- Dec. remainder _30'_	Dec. remainder _____	Dec. remainder _____

FROM HO 249

24- Hc _38°51'_ d _43_ z _134_	Hc _____ d ___ z ___	Hc _____ d ___ z ___
25- corr⊖ _22_ , Zn _226_	corr± _____ Zn _____	corr± _____ Zn _____
26- Hc _38°29.0_	Hc _____	Hc _____
27- Ho _38°20.1_	Ho _____	Ho _____
28- _8.9_ Ⓐ or T	A or T	A or T

Figure 35 A

59

ALTITUDE CORRECTION TABLES 35°-90°—MOON

App. Alt.	35°–39°	40°–44°	45°–49°	50°–54°	55°–59°	60°–64°	65°–69°	70°–74°	75°–79°	80°–84°	85°–89°	App. Alt.
	Corrⁿ	Corrⁿ	Corrⁿ	Corrⁿ	Corrⁿ	Corrⁿ	Corrⁿ	Corrⁿ	Corrⁿ	Corrⁿ	Corrⁿ	
00	35 56·5		45 50·5	50 46·9	55 43·1	60 39·?	65					
10	56·4		?·4	46·8	42·?							
20	56·3	53·?		46·7								
30	56·2	53·4										
40	56·2	53·3										
50	56·1	53·2	49·?									
00	36 56·0	41 53·1	46									
10	55·9	53·0										
20	55·8	52·9										
30	55·7	5?										
40	55·6											
50	55·5											
00	37 55·4											
10	55·3											
20	55·2											
30	55·1											
40	55·0											
50	55·0											
00	38 54·9											
10	54·8											
20	54·7											
30	54·6											
40	54·5											
50	54·4											
00	39 54·3											
10	54·2											
20	54·1											
30	54·0											
40	53·9											
50	53·8											

Here is the 35°, 39° App. Alt. column.

I find 37° here,

and 20 min. here. corr. = 55.2.

H.P.	L	U
54·0	1·1	1·7
54·3	1·4	1·8
54·6	1·7	2·0
54·9	2·0	2·2
55·2	2·3	2·3
55·5	2·7	2·5
55·8	3·0	2·6
56·1	3·3	2·8
56·4	3·6	2·9
56·7	3·9	3·1
57·0	4·3	3·2
57·3	4·6	3·4
57·6	4·9	3·6
57·9	5·2	3·7
58·2	5·5	3·9
58·5	5·9	4·0
58·8	6·2	4·2
59·1	6·5	4·3
59·4	6·8	4·5
59·7	7·1	4·6
60·0	7·5	4·8
60·3	7·8	5·0
60·6	8·1	5·1
60·9	8·4	5·3
61·2	8·7	5·4
61·5	9·1	5·6

My H.P of 57.7 is interpolated between the two H.P. figures here, for an answer of 5.0

Figure 35B

Back on the daily page, at the hour of our sight we find an H.P. factor of 57.7. I usually note this at the top of my work sheet because it will become a factor in my corr. for App. Alt. Meanwhile, go back to the very same column on the inside back-cover where we found our first correction. Straight down that column in the lower half of the page we find another column of figures headed by a boldface "L" and "U." These are for the Lower and the Upper limbs of the Moon. Ours was a lower limb shot so we will look down the "L" column until we find in the H.P. column to the left our number from the daily page of 57.7, or as close to it as we can. The closest number I find in my *Almanac* is 57.6, and the next number down is for an H.P. of 57.9. For correction I will interpolate between these at 5.0. I then scratched this at the top of my work sheet and added it to my main correction for a total of 60.2. If you read the short instructions on the Moon correction page you will see that all of these are added to App. Alt., but if you are sighting the upper limb, subtract 30 minutes from the answer.

Line 8—Now that we have finished and added corrections for App. Alt. we have our Ho at last. When you get used to it, it really goes quite fast.

Lines 9, 10, and 11 are treated as usual; i.e., correct your time and convert to GMT.

Lines 12, 13, and 14 (Dec.) are treated as usual except that you have a larger "d" to deal with.

Lines 15, 16, and 17 (GHA) are also treated like any other body that has a "v" factor. Here again it is a larger factor requiring more correction, but it is found just as any "v" or "d" is found.

You can follow the rest of the work sheet, and come to the same answer that I did with no unusual steps.

You will find my Moon shot plot at Fig. 35C.

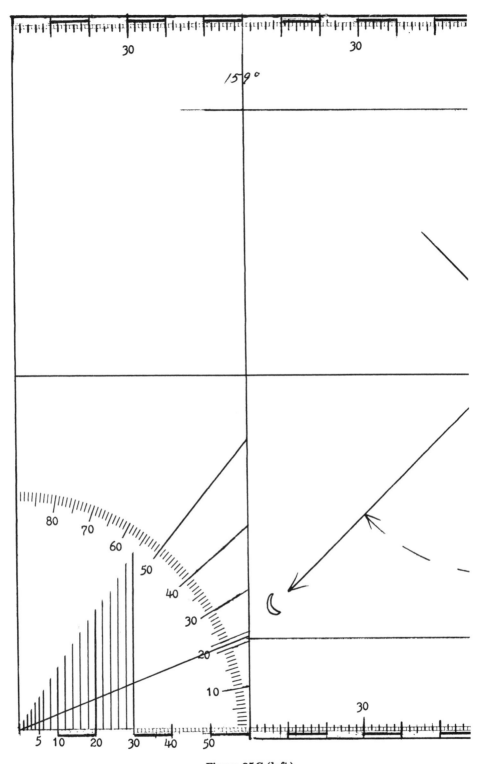

Figure 35C (left)

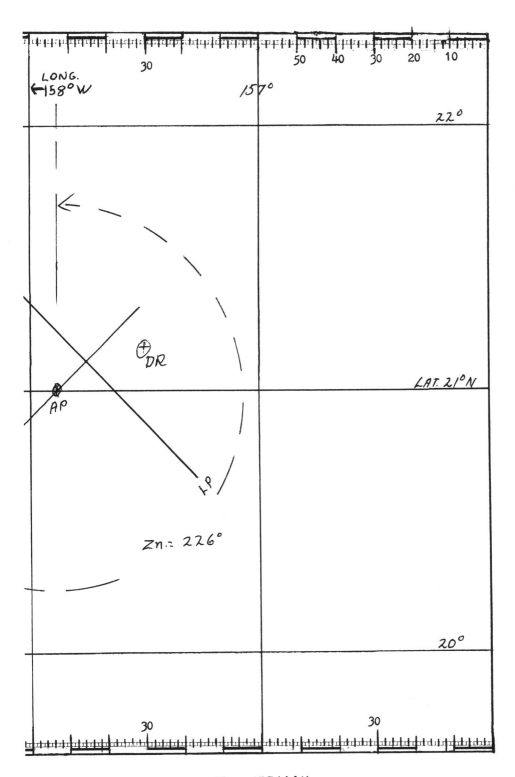

Figure 35C (right)

63

X. STARS

We come finally to star gazing, and if you live in the city, you would be amazed at how many stars there are out on a dark ocean away from all the electricity of the city sky. We will start with one particular star which we will treat separately from all the others because of its very handy position almost over the North Pole; POLARIS (The North Star).

We, in the Northern Hemisphere, are particularly blessed with this star. The Southern Hemisphere has nothing quite like it, at least at the present time, and as you will learn we won't have ours forever.

If Polaris were exactly over the North Pole (the axis of the turning Earth) it would give us an exact Latitude from our Ho. Said another way, our Ho would be our Latitude. From 45 degrees North Lat. Polaris would have an Ho of 45 degrees. From the North Pole it would be directly overhead at 90 degrees. Unfortunately, the North Star is a little off from North. It is about one degree away from the celestial pole, and thus, as the Earth turns, the Polar Star swings around this spot in the sky and if we used it without correction for Latitude, we could be off as much as one degree or 60 miles, and that's not very accurate navigation.

As I said, we will not always have a North Star, or at least not this one. The celestial pole is the place in the sky that Earth's North Pole points toward. The Earth is wobbling on its axis and its north pointer is inscribing a very large circle in the sky. In time this point will move on past Polaris and, perhaps some night far in the future another star will move into position and become a "North Star." I wouldn't worry though, for in our lifetime Polaris will be there since one swing around the circle in the sky will take the Earth about 26,000 years.

The question now is what do we do about that one degree circle that Polaris makes each 24 hours around the Celestial North Pole? Twice each day the Ho of Polaris does equal our Latitude (Fig. 36A) but also, twice each day it is a whole degree off, once too high, once too low. In between these times it is a constantly changing fraction of one degree. The last three white pages in the 1972 *Almanac* are devoted to helping us account for those fractions. To account for them we are going to that elusive character, Aries. You will remember that earlier I identified Aries as that point in the heavens in line with the Sun and the Earth at the time when the Sun first is at Dec. 0 during the year. This is the zero point for SHA, (Sidereal Hour Angle) the point from which the position of the stars is measured.

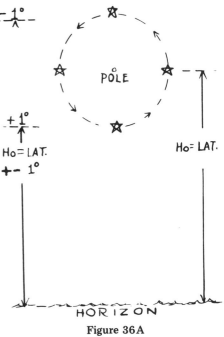

Figure 36A

64

The GHA of Aries is at the far left of each daily page, and the change in GHA for minutes and seconds of time is in a separate column on the minute pages. For a Latitude sight using Polaris you will need the LHA of Aries and this can be computed in the same way you computed in LHA sun or LHA planet.

Now, let's turn to the Polaris section in the back part of the *Almanac* and take a quick look at the layout of the pages.

Across the top of each page you can see that LHA Aries is divided into ten degree increments from 0 to 359. Each ten degree increment is divided into four sections as you run down the page. To the left of the first section are degrees from 1 to 10, and the figures in each column are in degrees and minutes to the tenth and are labeled "a_0" at the top of each column. To enter this table with, for example, an LHA Aries of 24° you would select the third column on the first page headed 20—29, and then go down the left hand column to 4 for your 24 degrees.

The columns in the second section down are headed "a_1" and you enter at the nearest Lat. in the left hand column to your DR Lat. No interpolation is necessary.

The third section down has columns headed "a_2" and you enter this table by the month in the left hand column.

The last section down is Azimuth, and it is also entered by Lat.

Now, look right under the Azimuth section; at the top of an explanatory paragraph you will see the formula we will use. It reads:

Latitude = Apparent altitude (corrected for refraction) $-1°$ $+a_0$ $+a_1$ $+a_2$

As far as we are concerned that means compute Ho for Polaris in the usual way, then subtract $1°$ and add the a_0 a_1 and a_2.

Let us go through a Polaris shot and make sure you have it. All we will need is the *Almanac*, no tables are necessary.

I am sailing from Boston to New York via Long Island Sound, and I am nearing the northeast entrance to the Sound as evening twilight approaches. I want to be at 41°05′ and a good check on Latitude will be very helpful.

My DR is: Lat. 41°05′ N. Long. 71°10′ W.

The date is: July 17, 1972.

The time: 8:20:10 (GMT 13:20:10)

No IC. No watch error.

HE = 9 feet.

Hs = 41°54.3′.

This is what the problem looks like as I work it out:

```
        Hs  =  41°54.3′
        Dip =  -   2.9
   App. Alt.   41°51.4′
     corr. -       1.1
        Ho  =  41°50.3′
```

From the daily and minute pages:

GHA ♈ hr.	130°26.9′	(♈ = symbol for Aries)
min.-sec.	5°03.3′	(from 20 min. page)
GHA ♈	135°30.2′	
D. R. Long.	71°10.0′ W	
	64°20.2′	(formula—minus west.)

POLARIS (POLE STAR) TABLES, 1972
FOR DETERMINING LATITUDE FROM SEXTANT ALTITUDE AND FOR AZIMUTH

L.H.A. ARIES	0°– 9°	10°– 19°	20°– 29°	30°– 39°	40°– 49°	50°– 59°	60°– 69°	70°– 79°	80°– 89°	90°– 99°	100°– 109°	110°– 119°
	a_0	a_0	a_0	a_0	a_0	a_0	a_0	a_0	a_0	a_0	a_0	a_0
0							0 13·7	0 18·8	0 25·0	0 32·3	0 40·4	0 49·1
1			Here, the 60°, 69° column.				14·2	19·3	25·7	33·1	41·3	50·0
2							14·6	19·9	26·4	33·9	42·1	50·9
3						·0	15·1	20·5	27·1	34·7	43·0	51·8
4	←	The 64th degree here,					15·6	21·1	27·8	35·5	43·9	52·7
5	(	and the a_0 corr here.					0 16·1	0 21·8	0 28·6	0 36·3	0 44·7	0 53·6
6							16·6	22·4	29·3	37·1	45·6	54·5
7							17·1	23·0	30·1	37·9	46·5	55·4
8							17·6	23·7	30·8	38·8	47·3	56·2
9							18·2	24·4	31·6	39·6	48·2	57·1
10							0 18·8	0 25·0	0 32·3	0 40·4	0 49·1	0 58·0

Lat.							a_1	a_1	a_1	a_1	a_1	a_1
°							′	′	′	′	′	′
0							0·5	0·4	0·3	0·2	0·2	0·1
10			a_1				·5	·4	·3	·3	·2	·2
20							·5	·4	·4	·3	·3	·3
30							·5	·5	·4	·4	·4	·4
40	←	Lat. 40° here, and the corr.				→	0·6	0·5	0·5	0·5	0·5	0·5
45							·6	·6	·6	·5	·5	·5
50							·6	·6	·6	·6	·6	·6
55							·6	·6	·7	·7	·7	·7
60							·7	·7	·7	·8	·8	·8
62							0·7	0·7	0·8	0·8	0·8	0·9
64							·7	·8	·8	·9	0·9	0·9
66							·7	·8	·9	0·9	1·0	1·0
68							0·8	0·8	0·9	1·0	1·1	1·1

Month							a_2	a_2	a_2	a_2	a_2	a_2
							′	′	′	′	′	′
Jan.							0·7	0·7	0·7	0·7	0·7	0·7
Feb.							·8	·8	·8	·8	·8	·8
Mar.							·8	·8	·9	·9	·9	0·9
Apr.			a_2				0·7	0·8	0·8	0·9	0·9	1·0
May							·5	·6	·7	·8	·8	0·9
June							·4	·5	·5	·6	·7	·8
July	←	Month of July here,					0·3	0·3	0·4	0·5	0·5	0·6
Aug.		and the corr. here.					·2	·3	·3	·3	·4	·4
Sept.							·3	·3	·3	·3	·3	·3
Oct.							0·4	0·3	0·3	0·3	0·3	0·2
Nov.							·5	·5	·4	·3	·3	·3
Dec.							0·7	0·6	0·5	0·5	0·4	0·3

Lat.				AZIMUTH								
°						°	°	°	°	°	°	°
0							359·5	359·4	359·3	359·2	359·2	359·1
20							359·5	359·4	359·3	359·2	359·1	359·1
40	←	For plotting, for Lat 40°				→	359·4	359·2	359·1	359·0	358·9	358·9
50		the azimuth is here.					359·2	359·1	358·9	358·8	358·7	358·7
55	·,	0 4	0 2	359 9	359 6	359 4	359·2	359·0	358·8	358·6	358·6	358·5
60	0·8	0·5	0·2	359·9	359·6	359·3	359·0	358·8	358·6	358·4	358·3	358·3
65	0·9	0·6	0·2	359·9	359·5	359·2	358·8	358·6	358·3	358·2	358·0	358·0

Latitude = Apparent altitude (corrected for refraction) $- 1° + a_0 + a_1 + a_2$

The table is entered with L.H.A. Aries to determine the column to be used; each column refers to a range of 10°. a_0 is taken, with mental interpolation, from the upper table with the units of L.H.A. Aries in degrees as argument; a_1, a_2 are taken, without interpolation, from the second and third tables with arguments latitude and month respectively. a_0, a_1, a_2 are always positive. The final table gives the azimuth of *Polaris*.

Figure 36B

You will note that in this instance, with Polaris, we use our D. R. longitude instead of an assumed longitude.

Now, to the Polaris pages (Fig. 36B) where I find the column headed 60°—69°, the seventh column from the left on the first page. Staying in that column I go down a_0 to "4" for 64° and read 0°15.6′ My LHA now, however includes an extra 20.2′, so I will interpolate between 0°15.6′ after the "4" and the 0°16.1′ after the "5". I round this off at an extra .2′ and take 0°15.8′ for my a_0 correction. On down the column to the next section at Lat. 40° I read 0.6′ for my a_1, and then down to the third section in the same column I read at the month of July, 0.3′ for my a_2. Now my problem looks like this:

$$
\begin{aligned}
\text{Ho} &= 41°50.3′ \\
\text{Minus} &\quad\; 1°00.0′ \\
\hline
&\quad 40°50.3′ \\
+a_0 &\qquad 15.8′ \\
+a_1 &\qquad\; 0.6′ \\
+a_2 &\qquad\; 0.3′ \\
\hline
&\quad 40°67.0′ \text{ or } 41°07.0′
\end{aligned}
$$

Let me call your attention to the a_0 section. You will note on studying it that the degree figure is not carried for all entries, but is implied as with Dec. on the daily pages.

XI. THE THREE STAR FIX

The honest-to-goodness, real, accurate FIX for the amateur at sea is the three star FIX at morning or evening twilight. The "pro" these days has an electronic "black box" of some kind that will give him the position of the ashtray on the bar if he wants it, by merely pushing the right buttons. Most of us amateurs are not so elegantly equipped.

We do have now, however, *H.O. 249 Vol. I*, and this is almost as easy to operate as a black box.

Learning to know the stars and to find them in the sky is a subject all by itself. Your *Almanac* is a good place to start, as there are star charts in the back, ahead of the minute pages that are much better than I can duplicate here. Also, H.O. Publication No. 9 *Bowditch* which I mentioned earlier has a beatuiful set of star charts with information on locating stars. You should really have a copy of this book. I'll get into the subject a little later, but for now let us get on with learning to use our *249 Vol. I*.

As we must enjoy our cruising, or we wouldn't be here, let us get to sea again with the snap of a finger and assume we are out of San Francisco on our way to Los Angeles. The first dawn is coming and we reckon we are off Monterey some little way out to sea (Fig. 37). In this work sheet note first the simplified form. You also will see some new symbols which I will explain as we come to them. Now proceed, line by line through our work sheet.

Line 1—This space is for the date, IC, and HE. A word of caution. If you change your position on the boat between sights and your HE changes, be sure to note it for that shot.

Line 2—The notation here is "Star finding data:" and, this is one of the advantages of *249 Vol. I*. Under this notation is a space for GMT, DR Lat., DR Long. (I have used the symbol for Long.) and for LHA Aries, and here again I have used the symbol for Aries. This is what you do for "star finding." Some time before twilight check in your *Almanac* to see when twilight will be and record that time in GMT in the first space. Then work out a DR Lat. and Long. for the time of twilight. Finally, compute LHA Aries for the anticipated time. With this information go into *249 Vol. I* first by Latitude, and second by LHA Aries. These are the only entering arguments. Latitude is both north and south: north in the first half of the book, south in the last half. All 360 degrees of LHA Aries are on double facing pages for each degree of Lat. They are arranged in groups of 15 degrees and have seven stars to select from in each group. The three which are recommended, because of their position, have an asterisk preceeding the name. First magnitude stars are in capital letters. At each entry, there is an Hc, and a Zn for the star at that LHA Aries.

Line 3—When you find the place for your Lat. and LHA Aries, copy the names of the stars as I have done.

Line 4—Then record the Hc and the Zn as I have on this line. When twilight comes, set your sextant to the Alt. for the first star (mine is Dubhe and the Alt. is 42°55′) and sight across the compass as indicated by the Zn,

WORK SHEET - HO 249 - STARS

1- Date _Nov. 9. 1972_ IC _+0.3_ HE _10 ft._

2- Star finding data:
  GMT _11:30_ DR L _36°50′ N_ DR λ _122°30′ W_ LHA ♈ _99°_

3- ★ _DUBHE_   ★ _SIRIUS_   ★ _MIRFAK_

4- Alt. _42°55′_ Zn _36_   Alt. _36°18′_ Zn _178_   Alt. _53°17′_ Zn _305_

5-	GMT _9_ d _11_ h _28_ m _10_ s	GMT _9_ d _11_ h _31_ m _45_ s	GMT _9_ d _11_ h _34_ m _20_ s
6-	Hs _42° 22.0′_	Hs _36° 37.1′_	Hs _53° 50.5′_
7-	IC Dip _− 02.8_	IC Dip _− 02.8_	IC Dip _− 02.8_
8-	App. Alt. _42° 19.2′_	App. Alt. _36° 34.3′_	App. Alt. _53° 47.7′_
9-	corr. _− 1.1_	corr. _− 1.3_	corr. _− .7_
10-	Ho _42° 18.1′_	Ho _36° 33.0′_	Ho _53° 47.0′_

Compute LHA Aries-- Rule: LHA = GHA - West, + East Long. Min.=0 W, 60 E.

11-	GHA♈dh _213° 42.9′_	GHA♈dh _213° 42.9′_	GHA♈dh _213° 42.9′_
12-	♈ms _7° 03.7_	♈ms _7 57.6_	♈ms _8 36.4_
13-	GHA♈ _220° 46.6′_	GHA♈ _221° 40.5′_	GHA♈ _222° 19.3′_
14-	Ass.λ _122° 46.6′_	Ass.λ _122° 40.5′_	Ass.λ _122° 19.3′_
15-	LHA♈ _98°_	LHA♈ _99°_	LHA♈ _100°_
16-	Ass. L _37° N_	Ass. L _37° N_	Ass. L _37° N_
17-	Hc _42° 27.0′_	Hc _36° 18.0′_	Hc _53° 38.0′_
18-	Ho _42° 18.1_	Ho _36° 33.0_	Ho _53° 47.0′_
19-	(A) or T _8.9_	A or (T) _15.0_	A or (T) _9.0_
20-	Zn _36°_	Zn _178°_	Zn _306°_

Figure 37

69

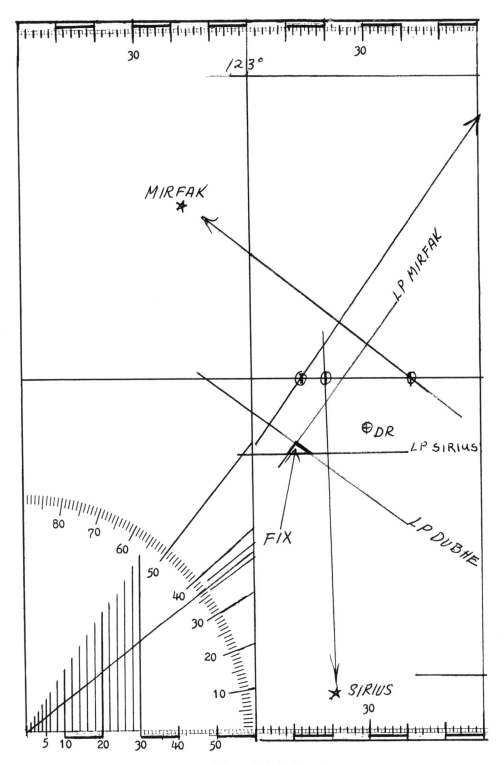

Figure 38A (left)

Figure 38A (right)

and there, very near the horizon will be Dubhe. No fuss, no bother. Just screw it up or down to the horizon, call "mark" to your helper to record the time, and you have it. Reset your sextant for the next star, check the new Zn and do it again, and then again for the third one.

Line 5—Is the exact time of each shot.

Line 6—The Hs.

Lines 7, 8, 9, and 10 correct each to an Ho. (Star column inside front cover.)

Lines 11, 12, and 13 are for GHA Aries from the daily and minute pages.

Line 14—A properly assumed Long. with the same minutes as in GHA Aries.

Line 15—Is the computed LHA Aries.

Line 16—Assumed Lat. (Whole degrees again.)

Line 17—The proper Hc from *249 Vol. I* for the final LHA Aries.

Line 18—Compare Ho with Hc.

Line 19—Indicate Away or Toward and the distance.

Line 20—Give the Zn for plotting. It may be the same as the first time, but if the time has changed enough (line 5) it will also change from the predicted time (line 2).

What could be more simple?

On Fig. 38A I have plotted the star shots computed in Fig. 37. Each is plotted just as the other bodies were plotted.

One additional note. My copy of *H.O. 249 Vol. I* says at the bottom of the title on the cover: EPOCH 1970. Because so much data is considered in advance before this book is printed, the tables have to be changed occasionally. In the meantime, to be accurate for years other than 1969 and 1970, correction of the final plot needs to be made. Table 5 in the back of the volume gives the correction by miles and direction. The instruction with the table is complete. My plot for example, is to be moved, according to Table 5, two miles on a bearing of 090 degrees. Take a good look at Table 5 and you'll see how it works.

Here is a practice problem for you. Work it out on scratch paper following the form of Fig. 37. I will give you the data you need from the '72 *Almanac*.

Date: Aug. 21, 1972		DR Lat. 10°40' N. Long. 76°45' W.	
Stars:	Capella	Achernar	Alpheratz
Time: (GMT)	10:04:35	10:05:40	10:07:41
Hs	44°31.0'	19°35.0'	46°22.0'
HE 8 feet. no IC or watch error.			
GHA Aries	120°58.3'	121°14.6'	121°45.0'
Answer:	1.8 mi. A	.5 mi. T	26.3 mi. T

Now, you fill in the blanks.

Let us make an assumption; one that I'm sure wouldn't happen to you. Let's assume that you went to sea and forgot your *H.O. 249 Vol. I* and then found that you really needed some star shots. If you remembered your *Vols. II* and *III* you can still get a star FIX.   *(Text continues on page 76.)*

```
GP h - 329° 31.9'            344° 34.3'            344° 34.3'
m-s   + 14 13.6              +    17.5             +    47.1
        343 45.5              344° 51.8             345° 21.4'
  ★   + 113 04.4             + 62 38.7             +146 23.8
        456 49.9'             407° 30.5'            491 45.2
  ★   -   360                -  360                -  360
         96° 49.9'              47° 30.5'            131° 45.2'
```

WORK SHEET ---------- SOLAR SYSTEM

DATE _Feb. 20, 1972_   MILES RUN LAST POSITION _____

COURSE _____   MILES MADE GOOD   _____

LOG _____   TOTAL MILES RUN   _____   MILES TO GO ____

1- DR Lat. _5° N_ DR Long. _84° W_ COMPUTED: Lat. _5° N_ Long. _84° 23' W_

2- IC _0_ HE _8'_	IC _0_ HE _8'_	IC _0_ HE _8'_
3- Body _ANTARES_	Body _ALTAIR_	Body _ARCTURUS_
4- Hs _56° 24.8'_	Hs _53° 14.5'_	Hs _41° 45.4'_
5- IC & HE _− 2.8_	IC & HE _− 2.8_	IC & HE _− 2.8_
6- App. Alt. _56° 22.0'_	App. Alt. _53° 11.7'_	App. Alt. _41° 42.6'_
7- corr. _− .6_	corr. _− .7_	corr. _− 1.1_
8- Ho _56° 21.4'_	Ho _53° 11.0'_	Ho _41° 41.5'_

TIME OF OBSERVATION

9- d h m s	d h m s	d h m s
10- watch corr. _____	watch corr. _____	watch corr. _____
11- GMT _20_ d _12_ h _56_ m _45_ s	GMT _20_ d _13_ h _01_ m _10_ s	GMT _20_ d _13_ h _03_ m _08_ s

DECLINATION --- FROM ALMANAC

12- mo.-day-hour ____	mo.-day-hour ____	mo.-day-hour ____
13- code d __ corr. ± __	code d __ corr. ± __	code d __ corr. ± __
14- DEC. _26° 22.4' S_	DEC. _8° 47.4 N_	DEC. _19° 19.3 N_

GHA ------------ FROM ALMANAC

15- mo.-day-hour ____	mo.-day-hour ____	mo.-day-hour ____
16- min.-sec. ____	min.-sec. ____	min.-sec. ____
17- code v __ corr± __	code v __ corr± __	code v __ corr± __
18- GHA _96° 49.9'_	GHA _47° 30.5'_	GHA _131° 45.2'_
19- Ass. Long. _84° 49.9_	Ass. Long. _84° 30.5_	Ass. Long. _84° 45.2_
20- LHA _12°_	LHA _323°_	LHA _47°_
21- Ass. Lat. _5° N_	Ass. Lat. _5° N_	Ass. Lat. _5° N_
22- Ass. Dec. _26°_ S	Ass. Dec. _8°_ N	Ass. Dec. _19°_ N
23- Dec. remainder _22.4'_	Dec. remainder _47.4'_	Dec. remainder _19.3'_

FROM HO 249

24- Hc _56° 53'_ d_55_ z _160_	Hc _53° 08'_ d _3_ z _83_	Hc _42° 08'_ d _12_ z _69_
25- corr⊕ _20_ , Zn _200_	corr⊕ _02_ Zn _83_	corr⊕ _04_ Zn _291_
26- Hc _56° 33.0'_	Hc _53° 06.0'_	Hc _42° 04.0_
27- Ho _56° 21.4'_	Ho _53° 11.0_	Ho _41 41.5_
28- _11.6_ (A) or T	_5.0_ A or (T)	_23.5_ (A) or T

Figure 38B

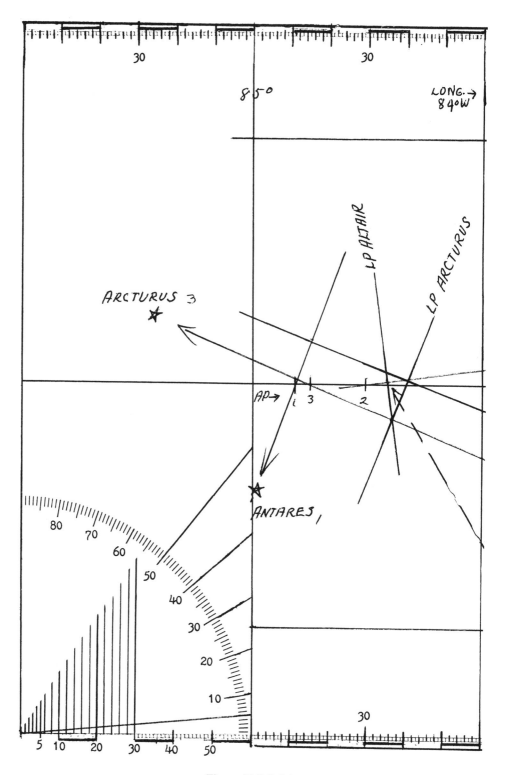

Figure 38C (left)

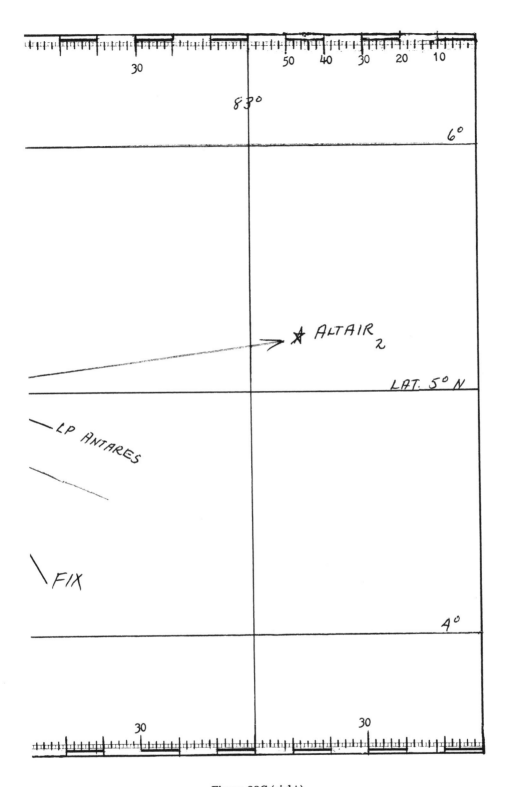

Figure 38C (right)

75

Let us say that you have cleared the Panama Canal from the Atlantic to the Pacific and that you are headed for the Galapagos Islands. You are not sure of currents, and there are some islands between you and your destination to which you want to give a wide berth. Night is approaching and the sky is clear. You are fortunate; you find three bright stars in the sky that you can recognize and they are all within the area between 30° north and 30° south declination. Your good fortune is because you won't always find the stars you know in this belt. You may be forced to learn some new stars. Volumes II and III cover only bodies in this range of declination.

You use your sextant, and within a few minutes you have brought down Antares, Altair and Arcturus to the horizon. You record the Hs and the time in GMT and grab a work sheet. Now let's go to Fig. 38B and see what you do with your information.

Lines 1 through 8 are as usual. You reduce your Hs to Ho as always.

Lines 9 and 10 are not needed because you were keeping a clock on GMT. Good work!

Line 11 shows your time so kept.

Lines 12 and 13 are also unnecessary. The Dec of a star changes so slowly that one figure is satisfactory over a period of several days. You will note that the Dec. of the selected stars is given with the SHA on each page in the *Almanac* for the period of three days.

I have also skipped lines 15 and 16 and moved to the top of the page where I worked out the GHA of each star. Do you remember the formula? GHA Aries + SHA star = GHA star. I looked up in the *Almanac* first, the GHA Aries for the date, Feb. 20, and the hour GHA Aries. I then turned to the minute pages and looked up the change for minutes and seconds, and added them for an accurate GHA. The SHA for the stars is, as I said, on the daily page for Feb. 20. I recorded that for each star and added it to the GHA Aries. My answer in each instance exceeded 360°, so I subtracted that amount for the final GHA star. I have recorded the answer on line 18.

The rest of the problem is then completed the same as any member of the solar system, that is, compute LHA, assume a Latitude and a Declination and record the Declination remainder. Complete lines 24 through 28 as usual.

The plot for this problem is shown in Fig. 38C.

XII. A START IN STAR FINDING

As I suggested earlier, there are a lot of good books on stars, and many ways to learn to identify them. To give you a start, however, here is the way I go about refreshing my memory.

I live in Honolulu, in an apartment building located at Lat. 21°18.8' North, and Long. 157°50.7' West, and I find that, from here, the North Celestial Pole and the area around it, is the place to start learning the heavens. In the first place it's important to be able to locate Polaris (the North Star) so that it will be handy for Latitude shots, and secondly, most of us, if we know any constellations, know Ursa Major even though we call it "The Big Dipper." I could never see the Bear in it anyway. (Ursa Major means the Big Bear.) Let us take a look at Fig. 39 and see what we can learn from a short course in this region.

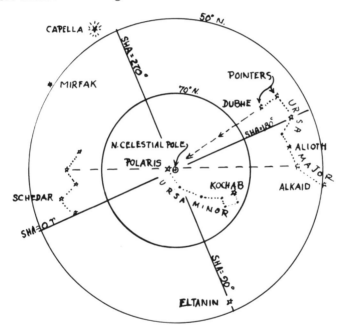

Figure 39

You will find the North Celestial Pole right in the center of the page and to its left, just off center, Polaris. The dashed line running across the page from the pole both ways marks the altitude of Polaris when it is at the same altitude as the Pole. Note that this line also lines up with the second star from the end of the "Dipper" handle and also with the second star from the small end of the constellation Cassiopea which is opposite the Dipper. This is good to remember as a part of "life boat" navigation when you may have lost your *Almanac*. Note next that Polaris is off center toward the star in Cassiopea. Thus, when Cassiopea is directly above Polaris, Lat. will equal Ho Polaris minus 1°, and conversely, when the star in the Dipper handle is directly above Polaris, Lat. will equal Ho Polaris plus 1°.

Remember that elusive first point of Aries, the zero SHA point? Cassiopea marks it for us with the last star on the big end of the elongated "W" (which she looks like to me). That star is called Caph, and it is actually at SHA 358 degrees plus. The star in the "cup" of the Dipper, opposite, marks SHA 180° (apx.). Next, the two stars at the upper end of the Dipper in this position, are the "pointers" that mark a line to Polaris. And last, there is the Little Dipper (Ursa Minor) with Polaris at the end of the handle, and Kochab at the other end. I can never really see much of a Little Dipper. The stars between Polaris and Kochab are too faint most of the time for me. Polaris and Kochab, however, are easy to find. There are few bright stars other than these in this near Polar area.

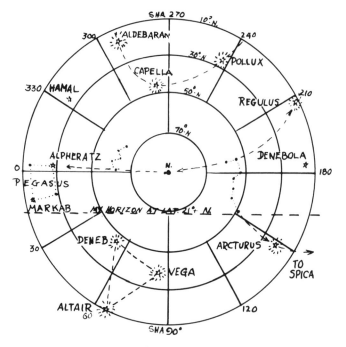

Figure 40

Now you can start learning the names of some of the stars. There are three in the Dipper that are named in this figure, one in Cassiopea, one in the Little Dipper, and a number scattered around that you may learn as they relate to these three constellations. Capella, near the top of the illustration is indicated as shining brightly. This is a first magnitude star.

In the next illustration, (Fig. 40) I have expanded the area of the sky to show what other stars you can find that also relate to the Polar region. Let us start at the Big Dipper. If you will find the two pointers again, but this time if you go away from the Pole in a gentle curve just a little further than the length of the Dipper, you will find a nice bright, first magnitude star, Regulus. Following the curve of the handle of the dipper outward a short way will lead to Arcturus, and then on further yet into the southern sky (not shown here) we will find the beauty, Spica. Both of these are first magnitude stars.

Now, let's see what we can find from Cassiopea. You will note that on a line from the Polar star across the small end of the "W" is a second magnitude star, Hamal, and across the large end of Cassiopea the constellation Pegasus with the star Alpheratz right in line. Markab is at the opposite corner of Pegasus.

As you may note, I learn some stars by the constellation of which they are a part, but others I associate in a different way. You will have to devise your own method, one which works best for you. An example of my association is the big triangle at the lower left of this illustration. Deneb, Vega and Altair are all members of different constellations, but I remember them as one big triangle following Arcturus around the sky.

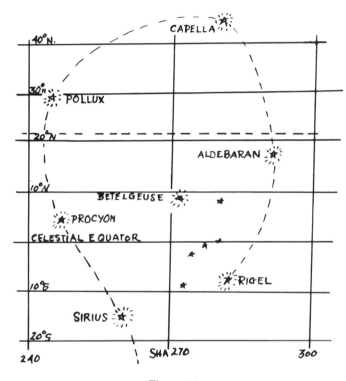

Figure 41

At the upper part of this illustration you will see my dashed line prescribing a portion of a large circle in the sky and passing through Aldabaran, Capella and Pollux. These are also members of separate constellations, but I associate them with the brightest spot in the sky (to me) the area around the constellation Orion which we will see in the next illustration. But before going to Orion note two other points of interest in the illustration we have before us. First, I have drawn a dashed line across the chart indicating my horizon here in Hawaii. The line is 21° below Polaris (my Latitude). The area above the line indicates the area of the sky that would be visible above the horizon with the outer circle of 10° N. actually 11° south of my Zenith. Holding this drawing toward the north, the stars would rise to the right (in the east) at the horizon line, and set to the left. The stars below the horizon line would not be visible to me at the time of this illustration.

Now let us move to my favorite piece of the sky, and it is a big piece. Figure 41 is the Orion I was talking about, and we are facing south as we are looking at him. From my position in Hawaii he is pretty high in the sky, and here is something else to remember for your life boat navigation. The star to the right, the leading star in Orion's three star belt, is exactly on the celestial equator marking it for you as Orion swings through the sky.

I think you can see now why I like this constellation. There are seven first magnitude stars in this one patch of sky, eight if you include Canopus further south, and I do. Sirius at the lower left of the page, is the brightest star in the heavens. If you notice anything brighter, it is either a planet, or an artificial satellite whirling around up there.

If you are interested in learning these stars by their constellation, your *Almanac* will provide you with the information you need. I associate them all with Orion and learned them like the numbers on a clock face.

Now, let's go to the next illustration (Fig. 42) and see another constellation that I am fond of. I like Scorpius, because it looks like a scorpion. It has

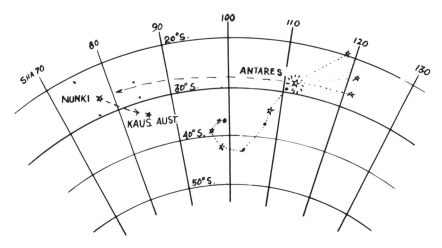

Figure 42

one bright eye, the first magnitude star Antares, and it also helps find two other useful stars in this otherwise relatively empty southern segment of sky. Nunki is behind Scorpio's head not quite two lengths of Scorpio's body, and halfway toward the tail from there is Kaus Australis. About two Scorpius lengths in front of the Scorpion, and twenty degrees nearer the celestial equator (almost), is "Spica." Spica is all alone in her little piece of sky, and very bright and nice. From my Latitude, there is one more bright star in the southern sky that deserves mention in this brief course, and it is "Fomalhaut." This star is at about the same altitude as Antares, and is a quarter of a sky behind at SHA 15 degrees. It will be high in the southern sky when Cassiopea is high in the northern sky.

I suppose that this course would not be complete without a look at the Southern Polar area, but for me it is strictly academic. I have not sailed in the deep south and the sky there is not familiar to me except as I see it from Hawaii. I can actually see all of the first magnitude stars in the southern area, but only when the sky is clear near the horizon. The dashed line across the chart in Fig. 43 will indicate my horizon, and as you can see, "Acrux" in the Southern Cross, as well as "Hadar" and "Rigil Kent", the most southern of these stars are about ten degrees above the horizon at their highest altitude from my vantage point. At the lower left-center, you can find Scorpius and locate the other stars we have talked about. (Remember, in the illustrations facing south, east is to the left and the stars will rise there and set to the right.)

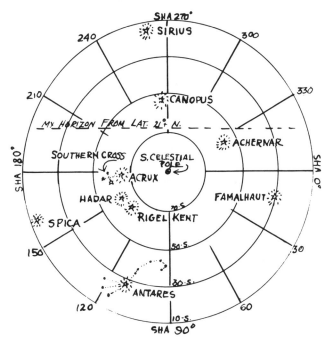

Figure 43

To help you locate all of these stars and constellations here is a guide. Check their SHA and then the following:

SHA# high in the sky at your Longitude at 8:00 p.m. during:

SHA#	
0°	Late December
90°	Late September
180°	Late June
270°	Late March

Remember, you can see half of the sky at a time so, if you're looking for a star a few months before the date shown, it will be rising in the east, and after that date, it will be going down in the west. The same is true for hours earlier or later than 8:00 p.m. Local time (Zone time).

So there you are, now go out and find them.

XIII. POLISHING YOUR SKILL

Let us start with a few things you don't really need to know in order to find out where you are.

There are those who say that unless you understand what is known as the "Navigational Triangle" you can't hope to be a successful navigator. I am not one of those, although I grant you will be a much better one if you do understand. I am very happy that those who put together the *H.O. 249* tables and the *Almanac* knew what they were doing and understood the math involved. They have done the geometry and the trigonometry for us and I for one have confidence in their work. Navigators of old had to know their math, and they frequently spent hours working out a position. The purist of today, perhaps, would like to know more just to improve his foundation knowledge. This is fine, but the aim of this manual is to aid the novice and not to frighten him off and thus encourage him to continue to follow airplane contrails to Hawaii.

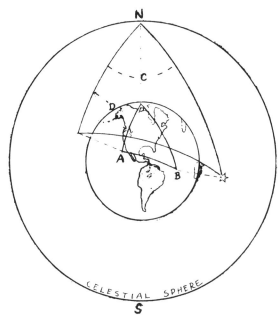

Figure 44A

For the curious, for the purist, for whomever, let's go to Fig. 44A and the Navigational Triangle. If you want to get further into the math of the problem, again I suggest *Bowditch*. This volume covers it completely. In this illustration I will just try to describe what the problem is.

In figure 44A let us say that our position is at "A" off the coast of southern California. "B" is the position of the Sun which we know by Dec. and GHA. "P" is the north pole. Projected above these points are the companion points on the celestial sphere. "C" is the angle between "A" and "B".

A good mathematician will tell you that with a triangle there are six dimensions, three sides and three angles. If any three of the six are known, the others can be found.

We know the length of side "A"-"P" as soon as we assume a Latitude. This is the Co- Latitude, or, the Latitude subtracted from 90°. We know the length of the side from "B" to "P", this is the Co-Dec., or the Dec. subtracted from 90°. We know angle "C" after we compute LHA. (In this instance the angle is LHA subtracted from 360°.)

With this information, the length of the side from "A" to "B" can be computed as can the angle "D". The length of the side is the distance from the GP of the sun to our position, and the angle "D" is the Azimuth to the body from our position.

Now let us look at the Navigational Triangle again. In our first view (Fig. 44A) we were viewing it from an imaginary distance in outer space. Here, in Fig. 44B we have another imaginary view. This time we will imagine that you

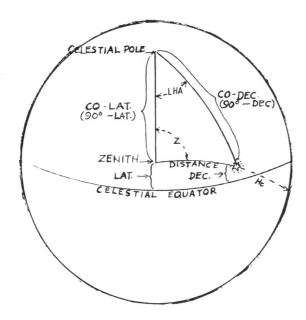

Figure 44B.

are somewhere at sea south of Hawaii at about Lat. 20° N. looking up at the dome of sky above. The circle around this illustration is the horizon. Directly overhead, at the center of the circle is your zenith. To the north, 20° above the horizon (the same as your Lat.) is the celestial north pole. To the west, and somewhat south, is the star Regulus at Dec. 12° N. (approximately). If you can imagine this, here again, then, is your triangle for that time, that place, and that star. The three corners are, your zenith, the pole, and the star. The three sides are the co- Lat., the co-Dec. and the distance from Regulus to your zenith. You can also identify Hc as the distance from the star to the horizon. Your Ho, of course, tells you where the star really is from your actual position. The difference between Hc and Ho being, as we have learned, the distance away from, or toward the star from our assumed position.

There are, of course, as many shapes and sizes of navigational triangles as there are places and positions for heavenly bodies to occupy, and they are all solved for you to the nearest minute of arc in your *H.O. 249* volumes.

Trigonometry may frighten you if you haven't studied it or haven't used it for a long time. It shouldn't. It involves looking up certain angles in a set of tables, finding certain values associated with these angles in the same tables and then following a formula through to a conclusion. (Of course, it can involve more than that, but what you need is about covered in that description.)

If you had no H.O. 249 tables, but instead, a set of "trig" tables with values for certain functions of the triangle you could find your own Hc and Zn. You would need trig. tables that list angles to the minute of arc, and include the values for: "sine" (sin), "cosine" (cos), and "secant" (sec). Since you would be multiplying five-digit numbers by five-digit numbers, a hand calculator would be nice to have, but you can do it with pencil and paper if you must.

Here is the formula for finding Hc:

When Dec. and Lat. are SAME name:
Sin Hc = Cos LHA x Cos Lat. x Cos Dec. + Sin Lat. x Sin Dec.
When Dec. and Lat. are CONTRARY name, change the plus (+) to a minus (-).

Here is the way this would work with the first problem involving line of position in this manual (that problem is Fig. 24). If you will look back at Fig. 24 you will see that I made the following determinations:

LHA = 303°

Lat. = 25°

Dec. = 22°01.7'

I now, go to the trig. tables and determine the following values for these angles (I interpolated for the .7).

		sin	cos
LHA	303°	0.83867	0.54464
Lat.	25°	0.42262	0.90631
Dec.	22°01.7'	0.37502	0.92714

I now follow the formula thus:
Cos LHA (.54464) x cos Lat. (.90631) = .49361 x cos Dec. (.92714) = .45764. Then I multiply: sin Lat. (.42262) x sin Dec. (.37502) = .15849.
Then I add: .45764
$$\frac{+\ .15849}{.61613}$$

I then look through the values for the angles under the heading sin, and find that the angle for which .61613 is the value (to the nearest minute) is 38°02', and this is the same Hc I found in *H.O. 249*.

Azimuth angle, which is the angle through east or west to 180°, can be found with this formula:

$$\text{Cos zn (Azimuth angle)} = \frac{\text{Sin D} - \text{Sin L} \times \text{Sin H}}{\text{Cos L} \times \text{Cos H}}$$

This requires a more complete knowledge of Trig. concerning the positive and negative values in the four quadrants of the 360 degree circle. There are, however, on the market these days electronic calculators that, when programmed properly, can do the job for you with the flick of a couple of fingers.

There are a few bits of information in the *Almanac* that may pique your curiosity. Let us look at some of them.

At the bottom of the columns on the daily pages are, other than the "d" and "v" factors, the following:

Under the Aries column, "Mer. Pass." and the time in hours and minutes to the tenth minute. Meridian Passage is the time of noon, for the Sun, or the moment when it is the highest, and due south, or north of you where ever you are. Every body in the sky passes your meridian at least once a day, and this is the time Aries passes. The time of noon is called Mer. Pass., or MP.

Under the list of stars you will find the SHA and MP for the planets.

Under the Sun column, as well as under the Moon column is the abbreviation, "S.D." and a number. There are three numbers under the Moon, one for each of the three days on the page. This stands for semi-diameter, or half the diameter of the body in minutes of arc. It changes from time to time because the distance of the body from the Earth changes.

Under the sunrise-sunset, moonrise-moonset data on the right of the right hand page are two small sections, one headed "SUN" the other "MOON". The section under Sun is headed "Eqn of Time" and Mer. Pass. You already know MP so let us examine the other. This stands for "Equation of Time". You will note that there is information for each of the three days on the page, for 00 hr. and for 12 hrs. Let me see if I can keep from confusing you as I try to say this simply. Equation of time has to do with the difference between where the Sun is, and where it would be if it were where mean time says it is. Did that do it?

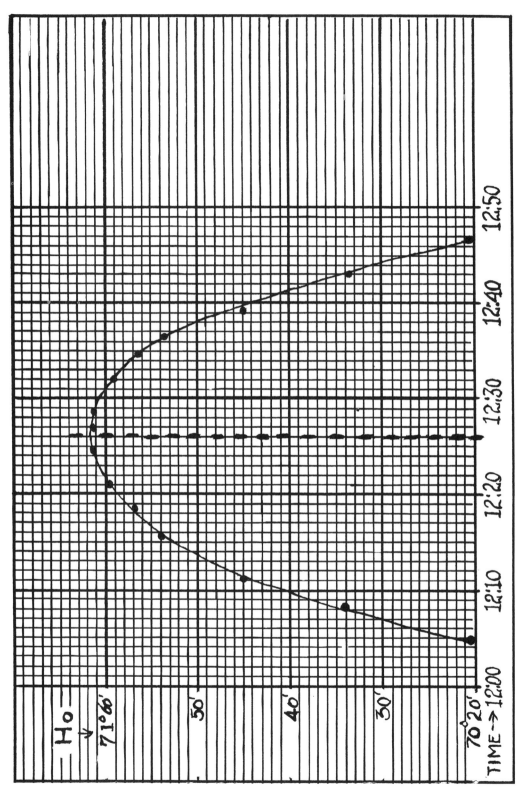

Figure 45

Let me try it another way. Theoretically, according to mean time (Greenwich), the Sun passes over the 180th degree of Long. at exactly 00:00:00 hrs., but, in fact, it does not. Sometimes it passes sooner, sometimes later. The minutes and seconds of time under the heading Eqn. of Time, gives you the amount of time before or after for the particular day. For example, let's take January 7, 1972. At 00 hrs. GMT the *Almanac* says that the GHA of the Sun is 178°33.0'. If I subtract this from 180°, I get 1°27.0'. Now, if I look in the minute pages I will find that the Sun will travel 1°27' in 5 minutes and 48 seconds. Down in the Eqn. of Time sect. for Jan 7, under 00 hrs. the time is given at 5 min. 47 sec. The one second of difference is a result of rounding off fractions.

The information under the Moon heading; I think, is self-explanatory, except that the "upper" refers to the time of passage at 0° Long. and the "lower" at the 180th degree.

Now, let us start refining some of the areas that we have already learned about. The most important, I think, is the Sun, and the time of noon, or MP.

The first time through, we learned to take a noon sight by watching until the Sun was at its highest, and then reducing that to a Latitude. At that time I said that you could get a rough Longitude by taking the midpoint in the time that the Sun lingered at the highest altitude and by looking up the GHA for that time. We can actually do a lot better than that if we wish. It is not easy to determine exactly how long the Sun lingers at the highest point.

There may be a time when we want something quite accurate. Take for example the situation, that the yacht Graybeard was in, during the 1971 Transpac race from Los Angeles to Honolulu. She was several hundred miles from Honolulu when her skeg carried away leaving a gaping hole in her bottom. It was midmorning, and she needed help badly. She called for pumps from the Coast Guard and gave her position. As I remember, and I was following the action, she refined her position several times during the next few hours. I don't know her navigator, nor do I know what he did, but he might have done one or all of the following, particularly if the time spanned the noon hour.

For this example, I went to the roof of my apartment building and shot the sights indicated in Fig. 45. You will note that this is an ordinary page of graph paper. I plotted the Hs on the vertical axis, and the time of the sights on the horizontal axis. I took, in all, fifteen sights. Next, I drew a free hand curve through what appeared to be the mean of the dots. Then, by measuring the width of the curve at several levels along its height, I found the center of the curve and drew it in at the 12th hr. and 26 min. I then looked up the GHA of the Sun at that time and found it to be 157°50.7', and that is exactly one tenth mile from my actual position.

To check that against the rough method, look at the three dots at the top of the curve. All three were at the same altitude reading, and the span of time was from 12:24:13 to 12:28:13. That's four minutes, and if I take half of that and add it to the first time I get 12:26:13 as the midpoint. The GHA of the Sun at this time puts me at 157°54', or 3.2 mi. away from the actual position.

I did one other thing. I shot the first sight at 12:05:05 at Hs 70°46.5'. Before the Sun got back down to that altitude again after MP, I reset the sextant at the same altitude and then waited until the Sun was on the

WORK SHEET ---------- SOLAR SYSTEM

DATE _July 27, 1972_ MILES RUN LAST POSITION _____
COURSE ___0_____ MILES MADE GOOD _____
LOG _____ TOTAL MILES RUN _____ MILES TO GO _____

1- DR Lat. _____ DR Long. _____ COMPUTED: Lat. _____ Long. _____

2- IC _0_ HE _300'_	IC _____ HE _____	IC _____ HE _____
3- Body _☉_	Body _☉_	Body _____
4- Hs _70° 22.2_	Hs _____	Hs _____
5- IC & HE – _17.1_	IC & HE _____	IC & HE _____
6- App. Alt. _70° 05.2_	App. Alt. _____	App. Alt. _____
7- corr. + _15.6_	corr. _____	corr. _____
8- Ho _70° 20.8_	Ho _70° 20.8_	Ho _____

TIME OF OBSERVATION

9- _27_ d _12_ h _05_ m _05_ s	_27_ d _12_ h _46_ m _43_ s	___ d ___ h ___ m ___ s
10- watch corr. _____	watch corr. _____	watch corr. _____
11- GMT _27_ d _22_ h _05_ m _05_ s	GMT _27_ d _22_ h _46_ m _43_ s	GMT ___ d ___ h ___ m ___ s

DECLINATION --- FROM ALMANAC

12- mo.-day-hour _2° 20.3 N_	mo.-day-hour _2° 20.3 N_	mo.-day-hour _____
13- code d _0.6_ corr. ⊕ _.1_	code d _0.6_ corr. ⊖ _.8_	code d ___ corr. ± ___
14- DEC. _2° 20.2'_	DEC. _2° 19.5'_	DEC. _____

GHA -----------FROM ALMANAC

15- mo.-day-hour _151° 20.7_	mo.-day-hour _151° 20.7_	mo.-day-hour _____
16- min.-sec. _1 16.3_	min.-sec. _11 40.8_	min.-sec. _____
17- code v ___ corr ± ___	code v ___ corr ± ___	code v ___ corr ± ___
18- GHA _152° 37.0_	GHA _163° 01.5_	GHA _____
19- Ass. Long. _157° 37.0'_	Ass. Long. _158° 01.5_	Ass. Long. _____
20- LHA _355°_	LHA _5°_	LHA _____
21- Ass. Lat. _21°_ N	Ass. Lat. _21°_ N	Ass. Lat. _____
22- Ass. Dec. _2°_ N	Ass. Dec. _2°_ N	Ass. Dec. _____
23- Dec. remainder _20.2'_	Dec. remainder _19.5'_	Dec. remainder _____

FROM HO 249

24- Hc _70° 23'_ d _58_ z _165_	Hc _70° 23'_ d _58_ z _165_	Hc _____ d ___ z ___
25- corr ⊕ _19_ Zn _165_	corr ⊕ _19_ Zn _195_	corr ± ___ Zn ___
26- Hc _70° 42.0_	Hc _70° 42.0_	Hc _____
27- Ho _70 20.8_	Ho _70 20.8_	Ho _____
28- _21.2_ (A) or T	_21.2_ (A) or T	A or T

Figure 46

88

horizon. At that moment I noted the exact time. It was 12:46:43. I then subtracted the first time from the second and divided the answer in half thus:

$$12:46:43$$
$$- \underline{12:05:05}$$
$$41:38 \div 2 = 20:49$$

Now, add this to the first time thus:

$$12:05:05$$
$$+ \underline{20:49}$$
$$12:25:54$$

This is the midpoint in the time span and the GHA of the Sun for this time is 157°49.5', or 1.2 mi. from my position on the roof.

Incidentally, the latitude sight put me directly on Lat. 21°18.8′ N. As you can see, several shots are better than one, particularly if you're in trouble or near an obstruction.

I did one other thing with that first and last shot, I computed them (Fig. 46) and then plotted them (Fig. 47). Let us take a look at the work sheet:

Line 2—Note my HE of 300 feet. This is the height of the roof of my apartment building, and you may wonder how I got the dip factor as it is not included in the *Almanac*. Here is the answer:

$$\text{Dip} = .97 \text{ x } \sqrt{\text{HE in feet}}$$

You should be able to follow the rest of the work sheet. The Hs is the same in both sights and so also is the Ho.

The time, of course, is different as is the Zn at the bottom of the sheet.

The LHA for the first shot is 355°, and for the second 5°, but note that these are at exactly the same place in *H.O. 249*.

The Dec. remainder is different, but the two are so close that they rounded off at the same place in table No. 5.

There is one other difference that brings up an important point in plotting. You will note on line 19 of the work sheet that I used 157° plus the minutes of GHA for my assumed Long. in the first sight, but for the second sight I moved it to 158°. (I plotted in dashed line what it would have been if I had used 157° as AP No. 2A.) I made this change because the line of position in a plot from 157° was too long. You will remember that a line of position, although plotted as a straight line, is actually a segment of a circle of position. The closer the body is to the observer, the smaller the circle, and therefore the better the chance of error with long lines. A safe rule would be to move your plot to the closest point to the intersection of lines with a sight at an Hs of 70° or higher. Any sight of 85° or over can, very likely, be drawn on the chart as a circle of position from the plotted GP of the body, but more about that later.

If you'll examine this plot you will see that the dashed line of Position would have been about a mile away from where the line from 158° intersected with the first sight line.

I have also drawn in the noon Lat. sight on this plot sheet for a three sight FIX.

Now, a final word about these equal altitude, pre and post noon shots. In the example I used here the Sun appeared to remain at the same altitude for several minutes. If the Sun's Dec. had been nearer my latitude the time would have been shorter. If it had been greater, it would have been longer. A look at *H.O. 249* to examine the Hc for LHA ranges next to zero LHA will give you the rate of Hc change between LHA degree changes. (One degree of LHA change takes four minutes.) This will give you an idea of the time you will have to plan for your shot.

Each summer, in May, the Sun passes directly over Honolulu as it's Dec. moves north to 23°+, and then it passes again in July as it heads back south for the winter. For a period of several months it is within 5° of our latitude.

The Sun, or any other body, is not easy to shoot when it is this near the zenith. It is difficult to find the low point when swinging the sextant to line up the object. The closer the object gets to the zenith, the longer the pendulum appears as it is swung. At one or two degrees away from the zenith you will have to turn from side to side as much as 180 degrees to find the low point. The Azimuth is also changing rapidly, and the low spot keeps moving. If you can overcome these problems, with practice, you can get a nice multi-line FIX without using the tables at all.

With the problem illustrated in Fig. 48, I assumed a position northwest of the Island of Hawaii at apx. Lat. 20°15' N. and Long. 156°30' W. It is a noon FIX. I first determined the time of noon at my position, then looked up the Dec. of the Sun for a span of some fifteen to twenty minutes over the noon period. I plotted the Dec. as a dashed line at 19°02.2' North at the time of noon. The difference in Dec. over the span of time is too small to plot.

Next, as the time of noon approached, I started taking sights at about four minute intervals. I recorded the time of the sights and the Hs. After the Sun had passed; after my last shot, I looked up the GHA for the time of each sight and recorded it on the plot sheet. I then marked in the Sun at each GHA position. You can see I used the symbol of the Sun for this marking. I next worked out an Ho for each sight and then computed the zenith distance just as in a regular noon sight. I then recorded each ZD. Finally, I measured off the ZD from the mileage scale and with a drafting compass drew in segments of a circle of position from each Sun position for my FIX.

This example illustrates the direct drafting of the circle of position I referred to earlier. The system might work for longer distances except for chart errors that would creep in. As suggested earlier, I wouldn't try it for more than 5° away from the body, but inside that range it is by far the best way to go about getting your FIX.

H.O. 214.

I learned navigation using *H.O. 214*, and still like it as a result. Now that *H.O. 229* is available, however, as a replacement for *H.O. 214*, the former publication will probably go out of print soon.

If *H.O. 214* is available to you and you want to use it, the conversion from what you have learned about *H.O. 249* is not difficult.

Here are the major differences:

One book of *H.O. 214* covers ten degrees of Latitude. The ten degrees are good for either North or South. It takes quite a library if you are sailing over a wide range of Latitudes.

The range of altitudes in *H.O. 214* does not go all the way down to the horizon. It starts and stops at altitudes of 5° above the horizon.

Declination in *H.O. 214* at the lower and mid-Latitudes is given for each degree and for intermediate 30-min. increments. In assuming a Dec. you assume the nearest lower entry and record your remainder from there.

When entering *H.O. 214*, you enter as you did in *H.O. 249* by Lat. first, then by Dec. The third entry, however, is by Hour Angle instead of by Local Hour Angle. The difference is this: in comparing your assumed Long. with GHA of the object, you assume minutes in the same way as in *H.O. 249* and then subtract the smaller of the two from the larger. The answer is the Hour Angle. In the eastern hemisphere a conversion of Long. has to be made to conform to GHA.

The figures at the entry in the tables are: first, the Hc as in *H.O. 249*, then there is a "delta d" ($\triangle$d), which is the same "d" that you have learned about. There is also a "delta t", but this can be ignored unless you want to plot from a DR position rather than from an Assumed Position. Finally, there is a column headed Az rather than Z as with *H.O. 249*. The Az is to be plotted from north, if you are in the north, through the east if the body has not passed your meridian, and through the west if it has. In the southern hemisphere the plot is from South through the east in the a.m., and through the west in the p.m. (The a.m. and p.m. is for the body you are plotting.)

The Dec. remainder in *H.O. 214* is figured to the tenth minute of arc and the correction tables are in the back of each book. You look up the correction for the full minutes first, and then the correction for the tenths and add them for the total correction.

When computing star sights, you first determine the GHA of Aries, and add it to the SHA of the star. The answer is the GHA star. From here, the star is computed just as the Sun or the planets. There is no "v" or "d" factor with a star.

H.O. 229

These are the newest tables and are published in volumes of fifteen degrees. One volume is larger than a *H.O. 214* volume and a complete library would be about the same size.

The major differences are:

The format has been changed completely. The first entry into the tables is by LHA. On each page the horizontal entry is Latitude, and the vertical entry is Declination.

The Azimuth angle is the same as with *H.O. 249* with the formula for conversion to Zn printed on each page.

Obviously, the LHA and its co-LHA are on the same page.

Information is provided for altitudes from horizon to horizon, and beyond.

Declination is given in full degrees as with *H.O. 249*. The Dec. remainder is corrected to the tenth minute and the tables for correction are in both the front and back of the book. The front section includes correction for a remainder of from 0.0' to 31.9' and the back section for 28.0' to 59.9'. These tables are more complex than either of the others, and take a little study.

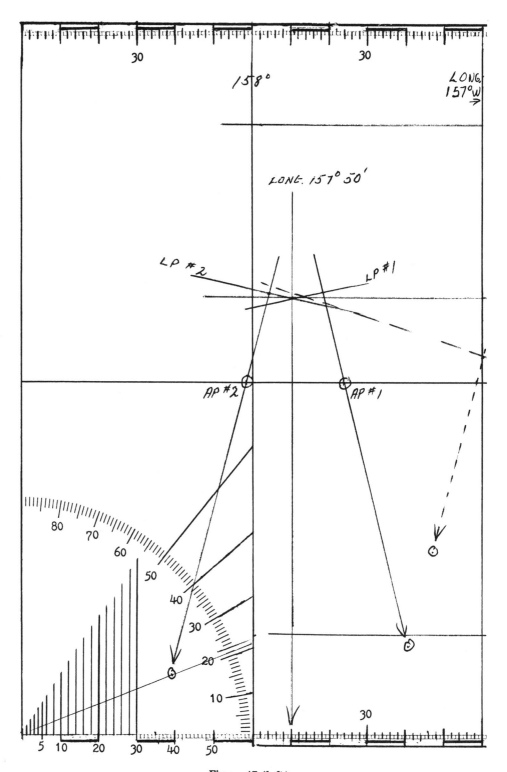

Figure 47 (left)

92

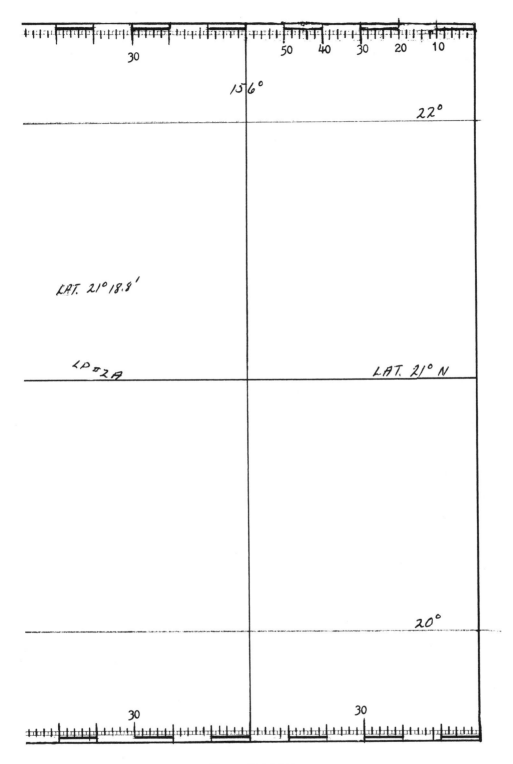

Figure 47 (right)

93

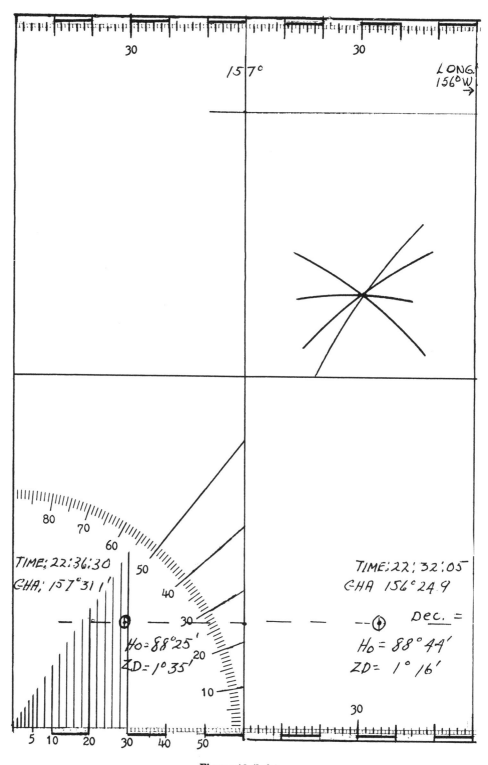

Figure 48 (left)

Note: The third position of the sun for the time 22:32:05, should be moved to the right ¼″ to correspond to the correct GHA for that time.

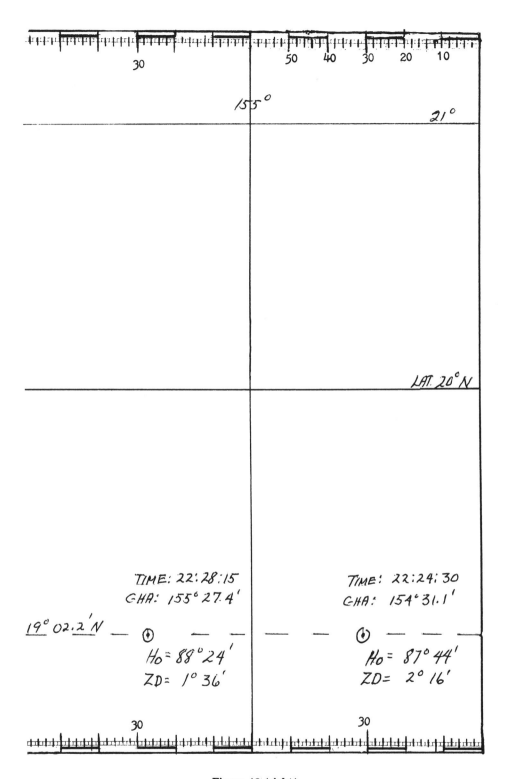

155°

21°

LAT. 20° N

TIME: 22:28:15
GHA: 155° 27.4'

19° 02.2' N

Ho = 88° 24'
ZD = 1° 36'

TIME: 22:24:30
GHA: 154° 31.1'

Ho = 87° 44'
ZD = 2° 16'

Figure 48 (right)

★　★　★

I was a bit "up tight." We were twelve days out of Los Angeles, the night was dark, and we were approaching the Molokai channel. We had been surrounded by squalls at sundown and I hadn't been able to get an evening FIX. I kept advancing my last Sun line and crossing it with radio bearings from Hilo and Kahului which were off to my left somewhere. I also had Makapuu radio on the nose, but it sure would have been nice if I had been able to see one of those mountains before dark. It wasn't to be, however. I now had to predict landfall and warn the crew to be on the lookout for the one light on Molokai which we could expect to see before we entered that ever-active slot between us and home.

It was nine p.m. Hawaiian time and I had to get some sleep as I'd been running a bit short of late. I went below and worked over my plots again and then called the crew together in the cockpit.

"We should see Kalaupapa light," I said, "about two points off the port bow by one a.m. If I'm asleep, wake me up." And then I went below again and crawled into my sack.

It had been quite an act. I was sure I had oozed confidence from every pore when I had made the prediction. Would that I had had reason to feel such confidence, but this was my first landfall of any consequence and, as I said, I was "up tight."

I slept fitfully for an hour and then felt my leg being shaken vigorously. It was my nephew Kevin.

"Wake up, Uncle Stu," he called, "we've got lights, and we've got traffic."

I scrambled from my quarter berth and dashed into the cockpit. I peered off to port and there, like two shining jewels nestled in cotton, were the lights of two small towns throwing their glow into the overhanging clouds. To the left of them an airport beacon was sweeping the sky with its beam. I watched for a moment in silence.

"Well," asked Kevin, "what is it?"

"The two towns are Kahului and Wailuku," I answered, "the rotating beacon is at the Kahului airport."

We were some thirty miles out, and I hadn't expected to see them through the squalls, but the clouds had lifted, and there they were fully as welcome as that mountain would have been.

We soon spotted and identified another rotating airport beacon up ahead, and with cross bearings on them, plotted our position. We were right where we were supposed to be, and a few hours later the Kalaupapa light came into view two points off the port bow right where it belonged.

It feels good, I assure you, real good, to make that landfall as expected. Now, get to work on your homework and join me out there.

END OF A BEGINNING

APPENDIX

TABLE OF FORMULAS

Relating to GHA and Longitude.
In the western hemisphere: GHA = Long.
In the eastern hemisphere: E. Long. = 360 – GHA

Local Hour Angle.

$$\text{LHA} = \text{GHA} \begin{array}{c} + \text{ east} \\ \text{longitude} \\ - \text{ west} \end{array} \quad \begin{array}{l} \text{east: minutes} = 60 \\ \\ \text{west: minutes} = 0 \end{array}$$

To find GHA of a star.
GHA Aries + SHA star = GHA star

Latitude formula.

$$\text{Lat.} = 90^\circ - \text{Ho} \begin{array}{c} + \text{ same} \\ \\ - \text{ contrary} \end{array} \text{declination}$$

Latitude formula when body is in our hemisphere
    but toward the pole from us.
90° – Ho = Zenith distance (ZD), Dec. – ZD = Lat.

Polaris latitude formula.
Lat. = Ho $- 1^\circ + a_0 + a_1 + a_2$

Finding Hc by use of trigonometry tables.
When Dec. and Lat. are SAME name:
Sin Hc = Cos LHA x Cos Lat. x Cos Dec. + Sin Lat. x Sin Dec.
When Dec. and Lat. are CONTRARY name: change plus to minus.

Finding Az, or Z by use of "trig" tables.
Sin Az = Sin LHA x Cos Dec. x Sec. Hc

Height of eye, Dip formula.
Dip = .97 x $\sqrt{\text{HE}}$ in feet

ABBREVIATIONS

A	Away (also, assumed)	Ho	Observed altitude
Alt.	Altitude	H.P.	Horizontal parallax
AP	Assumed position	Hs	Sextant altitude
App. Alt.	Apparent Altitude	IC	Index correction
apx.	Approximate	L	Lower limb (also, latitude)
a_0	First Polaris correction	Lat.	Latitude
a_1	Second Polaris correction	Long.	Longitude
a_2	Third Polaris correction	LHA	Local hour angle
Ass.	Assumed	LP.	Line of position
corr.	Correction	m	Minute of time
d	Day (also, declination correction)	MP	Meridian passage
Dec.	Declination	N	North
DLS	Daylight saving	s	Second of time
DR	Dead reckoned	S	South
E	East	S.D.	Semi-diameter
Fig.	Figure	SHA	Sidereal hour angle
GHA	Greenwich hour angle	T	Toward (also, true bearing)
GMT	Greenwich mean time	U	Upper limb
GP	Geographical position	v	GHA correction
h	Hour	W	West
Hc	Computed altitude	Z	Azimuth angle
HE	Height of eye	ZD	Zenith distance

Zn Bearing, true

SYMBOLS
(Used in Text)

o	Degree	$\math{(}$	Moon
,	Minute of arc	⊕	Position
=	Equals	♈	Aries
+	Plus	✵	Star
–	Minus	Aλ	Assumed Longitude
☉	Sun	√	Square root
♀	Venus	Δd	Delta d

(Other Useful Symbols)

⊕	Earth	♄	Saturn
♂	Mars	♃	Jupiter
"	Seconds of arc		